If . . . Then . . . Curriculum:
Assessment-Based Instruction, Grades K–2

Lucy Calkins with Elizabeth Moore
and Colleagues from the
Teachers College Reading and Writing Project

Photography by Peter Cunningham

Illustrations by Elizabeth Moore

HEINEMANN ◆ PORTSMOUTH, NH

To Brinton, Lily, and Jackson, my most important readers.—Beth

To Beth Moore, my co-author, with thanks for this book, and also for your contributions to so many of the books in this series.—Lucy

Heinemann
361 Hanover Street
Portsmouth, NH 03801–3912
www.heinemann.com

Offices and agents throughout the world

© 2015 by Lucy Calkins and Elizabeth Moore

The authors and publisher wish to thank those who have generously given permission to reprint borrowed material:

Cataloging-in-Publication data is on file with the Library of Congress.

ISBN-13: 978-0-325-07738-3

Series editorial team: Anna Gratz Cockerille, Karen Kawaguchi, Tracy Wells, Felicia O'Brien, Debra Doorack, Jean Lawler, Marielle Palombo, and Sue Paro
Production: Elizabeth Valway, David Stirling, and Abigail Heim
Cover and interior designs: Jenny Jensen Greenleaf
Photography: Peter Cunningham
Illustrations: Elizabeth Moore
Composition: Publishers' Design and Production Services, Inc.
Manufacturing: Steve Bernier

Printed in the United States of America on acid-free paper
19 18 17 16 15   EBM   2 3 4 5

Acknowledgments

THESE UNITS may appear shiny and new, but they actually represent the culmination of decades of work. Thanks go to the hundreds of teachers, coaches, administrators, staff developers, and kids who have had a hand in shaping them. Decades of trial and error have already taken place in order for us to arrive at the units you now hold in your hands. We're thankful to have been a part of that process.

The teaching captured in this book has been shaped in important ways by the leadership at TCRWP. Amanda Hartman shows primary teachers throughout the world what young kids can do as readers and writers. Spend a moment in a classroom with Amanda, and your teaching will never be the same. Many of the ideas on teaching reading that fill this series germinated from one of Kathleen Tolan's days in a school. She is always outgrowing her best thinking and taking the rest of us along with her. Laurie Pessah reminds each one of us that this work is all about relationships, trust, and dedication. Mary Ehrenworth pushes us to think critically and ask the right questions.

All the primary staff developers at the Project have contributed to these units of study, and we are grateful to each and every one. A special thanks to lead staff developers, including Shanna Schwartz, Christine Holley, and Natalie Louis. Julia Mooney has always been the guiding force behind much of the curriculum development at the Project, and we thank her.

This book also stands on the shoulders of decades of research and professional writing in the field of literacy education. The primary team at TCRWP is especially grateful to Marie Clay, Peter Johnston, Irene Fountas, Gay Su Pinnell, Elizabeth Sulzby, and Anne McGill Franzen. Our word study work owes an enormous debt to Donald Bear, Pat Cunningham, Isabel Beck, and Brenda Parkes. Traces of Tim Rasinski's important work on fluency can be found all over the units in this book. We thank Ellin Keene, Debbie Miller, Stephanie Harvey, and Anne Goudvis each for their influential works on reading comprehension. Lester Laminack has forever changed how we read aloud to children.

Our close friends and colleagues, Joe Yukish and Kathy Collins, have each influenced the teaching and writing in this book in more ways than they could possibly realize. You will hear echoes of their voices in all of these units.

The book could not exist without the amazing team at Heinemann. Special thanks to Felicia O'Brien, who edited this volume, providing guidance and an attention to detail that makes the world of difference. Thanks to Anna Gratz Cockerille for helping to oversee the process and for moral support as well. Thanks to Marielle Palombo and Jean Lawler for their unbelievable support.

Lucy would like to add a giant thank-you to Kate Montgomery, who taught me much of what I know about writing, and was my better writing-half for years and years.

Beth wants to add a special-thank you to her writing partners—Anna Gratz Cockerille, Stacey Shubitz, Tara Smith, Dana Murphy, and Betsy Hubbard. (Her writing life is forever changed thanks to you!) Lucy thanks them as well—your help with Beth's writing ended up helping the whole series.

—Beth Moore and Lucy Calkins

Contents

Kindergarten (Emergent Readers, Reading Levels below Level A)

Emergent Reading: Looking Closely at Familiar Texts • (Available in the Online Resources) ✴

IF your students are kindergartners who are emergent readers who could benefit from more emergent storybook reading, concepts about print, and developing letter/sound correspondence, THEN you may want to teach this unit after We Are Readers *(Unit 1).*

IF you teach first-graders and your assessments show that you have a group of students who are emergent readers (not yet reading level A, even with support), THEN then you may want to use this unit as ideas for small-group or conferring work with those readers alongside Building Good Reading Habits *(Unit 1).*

Kindergarten, First Grade, or Second Grade (Reading Levels C–G)

IF your students are kindergartners who are beginning readers who could benefit from reading nonfiction books, with an emphasis on learning a variety of topics and using new vocabulary, THEN you may want to teach this unit after Bigger Books, Bigger Reading Muscles *(Unit 3).*

IF your students are first-graders who are mostly emergent or beginning readers, THEN then you may want to use this unit as an extension of Learning about the World: Reading Nonfiction *(Unit 2). Or, IF you wish to teach two informational reading units, THEN you might teach this at the beginning of the year, and Unit 2 later in the year when students are reading at higher levels.*

IF you find that a group of your second-graders are reading at F/G during Becoming Experts: Reading Nonfiction *(Unit 2), THEN you may want to teach this unit alongside your nonfiction unit, or use this unit to guide your small-group work with those readers.*

This unit may also be an appropriate choice IF your second-graders are reading at levels E/F/G near the start of the year; you may want to insert this unit somewhere in the first half of the year.

Kindergarten or First Grade (Reading Levels C/D/E)

IF your students are kindergartners and could use some repeated practice with the print strategies in Bigger Books, Bigger Reading Muscles *(Unit 3), THEN you might teach this unit to extend that work.*

IF your first-graders need more support with print strategies after the first unit of study and are mostly reading levels C/D/E, THEN you may want to teach this unit following Building Good Reading Habits *(Unit 1), before diving into* Learning About the World: Reading Nonfiction *(Unit 2).*

Kindergarten, First Grade, or Second Grade (Reading Levels D–G)

Readers Get to Know Characters by Performing Their Books • 47

IF your kindergartners are conventional readers (levels D–G) and you would like to support comprehension work and high levels of engagement, THEN you might teach this unit after Becoming Avid Readers (Unit 4) as an extension of the character work that children are introduced to in that unit.

Another option for kindergartners is to use Bend IV of this unit as an extension to various "giving the gift of reading" lessons that briefly appear in other units (Units 2, 3, and 4). Giving the gift of reading involves teaching children to rehearse and prepare a read-aloud as a gift for others. IF you would like to include extra work on fluent and expressive reading in one of your existing units, THEN you might refer to Bend IV.

For first-graders, you may decide that you would like to teach a character unit early on in the year, while kids are reading mostly levels D–G, and then return to character study in Meeting Characters and Learning Lessons: A Study of Story Elements (Unit 4) later in the year when kids have moved several reading levels. Another option is to supplement Unit 4 using some of the bends in this unit, or use this unit as a guide for small-group work within your character unit.

IF you find that a group of your second-graders are reading at F/G during Series Book Clubs (Unit 4), THEN you may want to teach this unit alongside your series book club unit, or use this unit to guide your small-group work with those readers.

Kindergarten, First Grade, or Second Grade (Reading Levels E/F/G)

Word Detectives Use All They Know to Solve Words • 69

IF you teach kindergartners who are mostly moving into reading levels E/F/G, THEN you may want to teach this unit after Becoming Avid Readers (Unit 4). However, most kindergartners will probably benefit more from the "Readers Are Resourceful" unit (found in this book), which is also a foundational skills unit, but geared more toward emergent and beginning readers who are moving into reading levels A, B, C, and D.

IF you teach first-graders who are mostly reading levels E/F/G, and need additional support with print strategies at the start of the year, THEN you may want to teach this unit following Building Good Reading Habits (Unit 1), before diving into Learning About the World: Reading Nonfiction (Unit 2).

IF you find that a group of your second-graders are reading at F/G during Bigger Books Mean Amping Up Reading Power (Unit 3), THEN you may want to teach this unit as an extension—either by teaching this in its entirety, or selecting particular bends and adding them to Unit 3.

First or Second Grade (Reading Levels H–L)

Studying Characters and Their Stories • (Available in Online Resources) ☝

IF your students are first-graders who mostly read at levels H–L, THEN you might decide to teach this unit as an extension to Meeting Characters and Learning Lessons: A Study of Story Elements (Unit 4).

IF your students are second-graders who read at levels H–L early to mid-year, and your assessments show that character work (inference and interpretation especially) is a goal for many, THEN you may want to teach this unit following Becoming Experts: Reading Nonfiction (Unit 2). Teach this unit in the first half of the year to provide a balance of nonfiction and fiction, and to introduce the strategies students will need in their early chapter books, before diving into Series Book Clubs (Unit 4) in the spring.

First or Second Grade (Reading Levels J/K/L/M)

If you would like to return to nonfiction reading with your first-graders near the end of the year, when the majority of your first-graders are now reading higher levels than they were during Learning About the World: Reading Nonfiction *(Unit 2), THEN you may want to teach this unit near the end of the year as a return to informational reading.*

If you want to extend the work your second-graders began to do in Becoming Experts: Reading Nonfiction *(Unit 2), THEN this unit will provide more practice reading across texts—this time with a new spin—reading about and talking about nonfiction topics in clubs.*

First and Second Grade (Reading Levels J/K/L/M)

IF your first-graders are reading above the benchmark, THEN you may want to challenge them with this unit, which will involve reading books with rich literary language and vocabulary.

IF, after teaching your second-graders Series Book Clubs *(Unit 4), you find that your students could use more experience with a variety of genres, or that they could benefit from a focus on reading with drama and expression, THEN you may want to teach this unit.*

Introduction

CONSIDER THE LAST TIME you planned a big trip, perhaps a journey to visit family somewhere far away, or to travel to a conference, or even a field trip with your students. First, you had to determine what your main goals were. You probably had a list in mind of the things that were "must-do's," as well as the things that you wanted to do, but only if you had time or if the conditions allowed. If you were traveling with a group, then you needed to think about what would be best for the most people—knowing that it would be nearly impossible to please everybody all of the time. You then planned out your itinerary, making sure to schedule time for priorities, and leaving room for choices that depended on the weather and other factors, and making backup plans for the inevitable cancellation or change of plans.

Planning your yearlong curriculum is like planning a journey for your students. You'll need to decide on your priorities, as well as things that you hope to squeeze in. You'll need to consider all that you know about your students to determine what will make sense for your class as a community, and then make plans to differentiate for individuals and groups.

This is not to suggest that you are the cruise director, and your students are on vacation! They, too, will play a role in making the journey a success. By providing students with routines and choices and by working hard to create independent readers who are willing to work hard and make mistakes, you will help your students to invent their own strategies and ways of reading. Based on what you will observe students doing, you'll likely often say, "Holy moly, I need to change my minilesson for tomorrow, based on what these children are up to!" While you will have an overarching plan, you will also need to remain flexible, ready to modify the plan (but not abandon it completely) to respond to what your unique, quirky, independent children bring to the table each day.

Your curriculum planning is behind-the-scenes work, designed to bring together your community of readers so that while each is working on his or her own plans and goals, they are also all working on something together. In one unit, kindergartners will discover that they have superpowers as readers. In another unit, first-graders will become the characters in their stories, acting parts out and dramatizing scenes. In yet another unit of study, second-graders will become experts on topics that they read about in nonfiction books. All the while, each student will have choice over which books to place in his or her book baggie, in what order to read those books, on what strategies to apply (or not), on what to talk about, and more.

This book works as a guide for creating a yearlong curriculum. The table of contents for this book is much more than a listing of the chapters. Read closely and you'll see that it provides you with general advice that will help you make assessment-based decisions regarding your year of reading. Each of the units may work for kindergarten, first, or second grade, depending on the needs of your students. At the start of each unit you will also find an overview and introduction to the unit that provides further information on how to decide if that particular unit is right for your students, along with advice on assessment and getting ready for the unit (including materials, read-alouds, and shared reading). You'll also find resources to support these units as part of the online resources that accompany this series.

GATHERING RESOURCES IN PREPARATION FOR CURRICULUM PLANNING

Ideally, you will plan with your colleagues, working together across your grade level (or even multiple grade levels) to create a yearlong plan that makes sense. Rather than getting together, talking, and then retreating back to the classroom to create separate sets of plans, many teams of teachers find it helpful to do curriculum planning using one shared electronic document (such as Google Docs), where they can change and add to the plans together, plans that will serve as a guideline and resource for the group. The plans will become a living document, one that is revised and changed from year to year.

When you sit down to plan your curriculum, you'll want to have a sense of where your students stand in terms of reading levels, past experience with reading workshop, stamina and volume, exposure to various genres, as well as other assessment data: concepts about print, spelling stages, high-frequency words, and more. You can refer to Chapter 6 in *A Guide to the Reading Workshop, Primary Grades* for details on how to gather and analyze the data you will need for planning an assessment-based curriculum. Each unit in this book also includes a brief overview and assessment section describing what data you might want to consider before selecting that unit.

Next, you'll lay out your options for potential units, and the resources for planning them. When planning your curriculum, you'll want the four spiral-bound units of study from this series at hand: these represent what we consider to be some of the essentials of a yearlong progression of learning based on our experiences teaching in classrooms around the globe. Within each grade level you will see there is a balance between fiction and nonfiction, as well at least one foundational skills unit per grade. These units also align well with the sister series for writing workshop, Units of Study in Opinion, Information, and Narrative Writing.

UNITS OF STUDY BOOKS ACROSS THE GRADES

Kindergarten

Unit 1: *We Are Readers*

Unit 2: *Super Powers: Reading with Print Strategies and Sight Word Power*

Unit 3: *Bigger Books, Bigger Reading Muscles*

Unit 4: *Becoming Avid Readers*

First Grade

Unit 1: *Building Good Reading Habits*

Unit 2: *Learning About the World: Reading Nonfiction*

Unit 3: *Readers Have Big Jobs to Do: Fluency, Phonics, and Comprehension*

Unit 4: *Meeting Characters and Learning Lessons: A Study of Story Elements*

Second Grade

Unit 1: *Second-Grade Reading Growth Spurt*

Unit 2: *Becoming Experts: Reading Nonfiction*

Unit 3: *Bigger Books Mean Amping Up Reading Power*

Unit 4: *Series Book Clubs*

Consider these four units the frame around which to build your plans, but not the entirety of your curriculum. You will need to adapt, revise, and add to these, in order to build a plan that makes sense for you and your students, based on the data at hand.

In addition to these units, you'll also want to prepare for planning by having some familiarity with the options presented here, in the *If . . . Then . . . Curriculum: Assessment-Based Instruction, Grades K–2* guide. You may also want to consider units from the grade above and the grade below, as well as units of study and lessons contained in professional resources by literacy leaders such as Kathy Collins, Anne Goudvis, Debbie Miller, Stephanie Parsons, Tony Stead, Irene Fountas, Gay Su Pinnell, and others.

Once you've gathered your assessment data, as well as resources to draw from, you're ready to chart your course for the year.

USING ASSESSMENT DATA TO SELECT ALTERNATE UNITS OF STUDY FROM THIS GUIDE

The four essential units listed above can form the backbone, or the frame, from which you build your year around. You'll use your assessment data, as well as the interests of your students, to make decisions about the rest of the units you'll teach in a school year.

A few things to consider:

- What skills and strategies are children beginning the school year with? What do you hope they will leave with?

- What genres and types of books do you hope to share with your students?

- What are your goals for this year of reading?

You'll need to look across your data, culling the information, thinking, "What do my students already know? What can they already do?" Then ask yourself, "What do I want them to know? What do I want them to be able to do?" You'll look to rigorous national and international standards, you'll call upon your experiences in the classroom and as a reader yourself, you'll collaborate with colleagues, and you'll set high, but attainable goals. You can refer to Chapter 6 in the *Guide to the Reading Workshop, Primary Grades* for details on the types of assessments you will want to consider, as well as advice on how to administer and analyze these assessments.

You'll then set about creating an itinerary for your year of reading that starts where your students are, and takes them to where you'd like them to be. At five or six weeks a unit, most teachers plan on six to eight units per year. This means you might select two to four additional units to fill out your school year. In this book you will find alternate units that you can choose from to create a yearlong curriculum that meets the needs of your students.

There are several ways you might use assessment data to plan ahead for the year to come. One is to look at the incoming group of students and any information you can glean from last year's teachers (or in the case of kindergartners, if your school does any kind of kindergarten screening, you might use what you can from that). You will also want to reflect on your own past experiences as well: What did you learn about the units from your experience teaching this year's kids (and last year's, and in all the year's before)? You can use past years' data to anticipate what the incoming reading levels will likely be, as well as predictable issues and potential solutions within each unit.

EXAMPLES OF ASSESSMENT-BASED YEARLONG CURRICULUM CALENDARS

What do you plan to teach this year? What genres and text types will your students need to experience? How many weeks will each unit last? In the spring, will you plan to revisit some of the teaching you did in the fall? Are there units that you could include in the fall that would support the work you anticipate wanting to do in the spring? The document you create will serve as a map for you to navigate as your year unfolds.

Use past year's data to anticipate what to expect this year.

In the example that follows, kindergarten teachers planned together, knowing that year after year, their students tend to come with very little literacy experience outside of school, with very few of their children having attended preschool. Knowing this, they planned to add "Emergent Reading: Looking Closely at Familiar Texts" in between the Unit 1 and Unit 2 books to give children extra experience with storytelling, phonemic awareness, letter-sound correspondence, and early reading behaviors. They used past year's assessment data to anticipate what levels their students would likely be reading across the year, and planned accordingly, also aiming to include a balance of fiction and nonfiction in their calendar.

If you teach kindergarten, and your class has a similar profile to the class discussed here, we strongly recommend that you add this unit to your curricular plan as well, preferably before the *Super Powers* unit. Doing so will ensure that your *Super Powers* unit will be as successful as possible. You can access this unit via the online resources for this book.

We Are Readers (Unit 1)

"Emergent Reading: Looking Closely at Familiar Texts"

Super Powers: Reading with Print Strategies and Sight Word Power (Unit 2)

Bigger Books, Bigger Reading Muscles (Unit 3)

"Growing Expertise in Little Books: Nonfiction Reading" (*If . . . Then . . . Curriculum*)

Becoming Avid Readers (Unit 4)

"Readers Get to Know Characters by Performing Their Books" (*If . . . Then . . . Curriculum*)

Plan for a curriculum that provides repeated practice, with a balance of text types and units focusing on different skills and strategies.

The next example, from first grade, demonstrates how you might use the *If . . . Then . . . Curriculum* to plan a calendar that includes two character units, two nonfiction units, and two foundational skills units—a calendar that repeats the cycle to give kids repeated practice with similar skills and strategies (though they will change accordingly as children's reading levels will have changed). This allows students to experience all types of texts in the fall, and again in the spring when they have grown as readers.

Building Good Reading Habits (Unit 1)

"Word Detectives Use All They Know to Solve Words" (*If . . . Then . . . Curriculum*)

Learning About the World: Reading Nonfiction (Unit 2)

"Readers Get to Know Characters by Performing Their Books" (*If . . . Then . . . Curriculum*)

Readers Have Big Jobs to Do: Fluency, Phonics, and Comprehension (Unit 3)

Meeting Characters and Learning Lessons: A Study of Story Elements (Unit 4)

Reading Nonfiction Cover to Cover: Nonfiction Book Clubs (*If . . . Then . . . Curriculum*)

Look across more than one grade level to meet your students' needs.

In the example that follows, this first-grade team knew that many of their incoming students had ended kindergarten well below the benchmark, not yet reading level D books. Anticipating that many of their children would experience "summer slide" (a phenomenon that involves loss of reading stamina along with slipping back a few reading levels), they decided to adjust their curriculum so that the first unit would include emergent reading, and that the school year would provide the necessary support to have most of their children reading at the benchmark levels by the end of first grade. To support this work, they also planned an extra reading time each day to provide intervention and extra time for reading for all their students.

Building Good Reading Habits (Unit 1), supplemented with "Emergent Reading: Looking Closely at Familiar Texts" (*If . . . Then . . . Curriculum* Online Resources) and *We Are Readers* (Kindergarten, Unit 1)

"Readers Are Resourceful: Tackling Hard Words and Tricky Parts in Books" (*If . . . Then . . . Curriculum*), supplemented with *Super Powers: Reading with Print Strategies and Sight Word Power* (Kindergarten, Unit 2), and *Bigger Books, Bigger Reading Muscles* (Kindergarten, Unit 3)

Learning About the World: Reading Nonfiction (Unit 2), supplemented with "Growing Expertise in Little Books: Nonfiction Reading" (*If . . . Then . . . Curriculum*)

"Word Detectives Use All They Know to Solve Words" (*If . . . Then . . . Curriculum*)

"Readers Get to Know Characters by Performing Their Books" (*If . . . Then . . . Curriculum*)

Readers Have Big Jobs to Do: Fluency, Phonics, and Comprehension (Unit 3)

Meeting Characters and Learning Lessons: A Study of Story Elements (Unit 4), supplemented with "Studying Characters and Their Stories" (*If . . . Then . . . Curriculum* Online Resources)

Plan backwards by thinking about your end-of-year goals first, then build up to them.

Here is a second-grade plan that reflects thoughtful planning by thinking about the end of the year and moving backward from there. The teachers decided to plan for *Series Book Clubs* (Unit 4) not to finish the year, but a little earlier, leaving time to return to nonfiction at the end of the year, when their students are reading at higher levels. These teachers also noticed that in the past, students' reading volume tended to dip during nonfiction units. Therefore, they decided not to end the year with nonfiction, but instead with "Reading and Role-Playing: Fairy Tales, Folktales, Fables, and Fantasy" (*If . . . Then . . . Curriculum*). The return to character and story elements in this unit tends to involve high levels of engagement, with students reading a very high volume and with stamina (a great way to end the year), as well as giving them opportunities for sophisticated comprehension work and plenty of vocabulary and language to study.

Second-Grade Reading Growth Spurt (Unit 1)

Becoming Experts: Reading Nonfiction (Unit 2)

"Studying Characters and Their Stories" (*If . . . Then . . . Curriculum* Online Resources)

Bigger Books Mean Amping Up Reading Power (Unit 3)

Series Book Clubs (Unit 4)

"Reading Nonfiction Cover to Cover: Nonfiction Book Clubs" (*If . . . Then . . . Curriculum*)

"Reading and Role-Playing: Fairy Tales, Folktales, Fables, and Fantasy" (*If . . . Then . . . Curriculum*)

Utilize the units of study spiral-bound books and the *If . . . Then . . . Curriculum* book for multiage/multigrade classrooms.

This next example reflects that the minilessons in every book may be geared to grade-level standards but are actually multilevel in many ways, often transferable to other grades. This group of first-second-grade multiage teachers utilized the units from both grade levels and the *If . . . Then . . . Curriculum* units, knowing that the work in those books would apply to all their learners, so long as they looked to the small-group work sections within each book and differentiated for students reading at different reading levels.

Second-Grade Reading Growth Spurt (Grade 2, Unit 1), supplemented with *Building Good Reading Habits* (Grade 1, Unit 1)

"Word Detectives Use All They Know to Solve Words" (*If . . . Then . . . Curriculum*)

"Studying Characters and Their Stories" (*If . . . Then . . . Curriculum* Online Resources) 👆

Becoming Experts: Reading Nonfiction (Grade 2, Unit 2), supplemented with *Learning About the World: Reading Nonfiction* (Grade 1, Unit 2)

Bigger Books Mean Amping Up Reading Power (Grade 2, Unit 3), supplemented with *Readers Have Big Jobs to Do: Fluency, Phonics, and Comprehension* (Grade 1, Unit 3)

Series Book Clubs (Grade 2, Unit 4), supplemented with *Meeting Characters and Learning Lessons: A Study of Story Elements* (Grade 1, Unit 4)

"Reading Nonfiction Cover to Cover: Nonfiction Book Clubs" (*If . . . Then . . . Curriculum*)

While units may focus on different topics (e.g., foundational skills or reading nonfiction), each unit builds upon a set of reading skills that are explicitly developed throughout the units and across the grades, such as monitoring for sense, cross checking, and reading with phrasing. Specific skills may be highlighted more in some units than in others, but all will be reinforced multiple times in a variety of contexts. The units of study in this series work as a spiraling curriculum. Students are given opportunities time and time again to return to similar work with a new lens and while reading books at new levels of text complexity.

Know that each unit in the K–2 series is planned with a particular range of text complexity in mind, and with readers in various stages of development. As you plan your course of study for the year, you will want to use your assessment data to make sure that the units you select match the stages and reading levels of your students.

We suggest planning for a roughly equal division of fiction and nonfiction units, although a number of units straddle those categories. For example, during most foundational skills units, children are reading a mix of both fiction and nonfiction just-right texts. Further, some units support students working in partnerships, while others support thinking and talking across loosely connected books with a reading club. When a unit supports partnerships, this usually means that the reading workshop shifts midway through the workshop to allow for partners to read and talk together. Often there are also partner conversations during the minilesson or during a mid-workshop teaching. During units that support clubs, readers meet to read and talk in groups of four rather than in pairs. As you plan your yearlong curriculum, you will want to preview the units to see if students are working in partnerships or clubs.

You'll also need to plan the approximate dates for each unit, so that as your year begins, you can pace yourself accordingly and align your teaching with writing and other subject areas whenever it makes sense to do so. Some schools provide a centrally located calendar in the main office, school library, or teachers' room, so that you can easily see when your colleagues will be celebrating their reading and writing units; you can coordinate celebrations more easily. Imagine, instead of having to go door to door to find out when others will be holding their reading and writing celebrations, you could just check the calendar and leave a note for others to see.

More than that, committing to an end date for each of your units helps you plan your pacing strategically, keeping the big picture of your entire year in mind as you decide how much time to devote to each unit of study. The launch of each new unit breathes life into your classroom, builds anticipation and excitement about reading, and contributes to an overarching goal for the year: growing lifelong readers. If a unit stretches on too long (more than six weeks is probably too long), not only does that mean less time for studying other genres, text types, skills and strategies, but it also means your students' engagement is bound to falter. Months of the same unit can feel like an eternity to a small child. If kids' aren't fully engaged, then their learning suffers.

Finally, as part of your planning process, you'll imagine how to create classrooms, and indeed a whole school, where reading is something children choose to do, rather than something they simply have to do. You'll look at your classroom libraries and take stock, thinking about what topics, genres, authors, and text types you want to add to your wish-lists, as well as how to organize classroom libraries to attract kids to books. You'll consider your read-alouds and your shared reading selections and how to use those to catapult your kids' love of books. You'll consider even the walls of your classroom, and make some plans for how you might display authentic student work (rather than prepackaged posters) that sends the message proudly: we are readers and writers. We work hard and make mistakes in this classroom. We are *all* readers and writers in here. First make some general plans for how you will immerse your kids in the reading life. Then set about planning your units of study across the year.

Kindergarten, First Grade, or Second Grade

Growing Expertise in Little Books

Nonfiction Reading

RATIONALE/INTRODUCTION

Children are just beginning to explore the wideness of the world, to see that there are wonders much bigger than their own inventions. It's thrilling to watch a six-year-old ask how a rainbow is made or where air comes from, and listen, rapt, to our answers. But with those questions comes a big responsibility. As teachers, it rests on our shoulders to continue to pique our little learners' curiosities, giving them experiences that will foster this beyond-the-horizon learning. When we take children to the zoo or the park, or when we give them a role in the weekly household laundry, we are not merely spending time with them or getting work done, we are also teaching them to read, think, and learn about the world.

There may be a number of scenarios where you would want to include this unit in your yearlong curriculum plans. This is a unit designed for beginning readers (reading levels C–G), meant to provide instruction in the skills and strategies that will help move them from simple books about familiar topics, with a line or two of text per page, into increasingly complex information books with less picture support, more lines of text, and new vocabulary to learn. The informational books beginning readers are holding may look simple enough—but don't be deceived. There are topics to study, information to gather, and ideas to be had.

Kindergartners will be introduced to nonfiction books in various ways in other units. Of course, many of the list books and pattern books kindergartners have been reading all along may qualify as "informational." While other units just touch on nonfiction reading, this unit will immerse your young readers in the world of informational reading for several weeks, giving them plenty of opportunity for repeated practice, and mastery of skills that are particular to reading nonfiction. This unit builds nicely off of the work of *Bigger Books, Bigger Reading Muscles* (Unit 3) and will provide the perfect opportunity for kids to apply all of the foundational skills they worked hard on in that unit.

This unit might also serve as a complement to the first-grade unit of study, *Learning About the World: Reading Nonfiction* (Unit 2). You'll find that the first two bends in this unit overlap nicely with the bends in the first-grade unit, so that you can use the work found here as extra support for those bends. The third bend in this unit will provide instruction with compare and contrast, a nice addition to your nonfiction unit. Another possibility for first-graders is for this unit to serve as an early-in-the-year nonfiction reading unit, when children are still reading at beginning reading levels; then *Learning About the World: Reading Nonfiction* would serve as a second later-in-the-year unit of study, when children have moved several levels and are reading more complex texts.

Lastly, if you find that a group of your second-graders are reading at levels E/F/G during *Becoming Experts: Reading Nonfiction* (Unit 2), then you may want to teach parts of this unit alongside your nonfiction unit, or use this unit to guide your small-group work with those readers. This unit may also be an appropriate choice if your second-graders are reading at levels E/F/G near the start of the year, and you plan to teach *Becoming Experts: Reading Nonfiction* later in the year.

No matter the grade level, this is a unit on nonfiction reading for beginning readers, and we want to keep that sense of learning and information alive for this unit. However, we recognize that many of the books your children may be reading (levels A–G) are list-type books, or pattern books, that are neither fiction nor nonfiction. This unit emphasizes the importance of learning from books. This will mean teaching children to ponder what their books are about and to read closely, looking for new ideas, information, and vocabulary on every page. We believe that even these beginning-level books hold newness and wonder for youngsters. After all, we take these same children on walks around their own neighborhoods and invite them to see and learn something new—why shouldn't they do the same with their books? So, in this unit, we invite you to both make big what may seem ordinary and help your students marvel at all they can learn from the books in their hands.

When we teach children to think and speak in ways that help them make sense of their experiences— to use particular words and technical vocabulary to talk about activities, places, or topics—we not only bolster their knowledge of the world but also arm them with the language to present knowledge and ideas. Through building on each other's ideas, articulating their own ideas, and confirming that they have been understood, children gain command of Standard English and start to use wide-ranging vocabulary. This kind of conversation also helps ELLs develop their understanding of context and content. More broadly, by extending strategies and information that they know from one topic to another and from one part of their day to another, children become self-directed learners who are high-level strategic thinkers and *problem solvers*.

As this unit begins, you will invite your students to notice all of the details in their books and encourage them to pull back after reading to answer questions like: *What was this book about? What did it teach me? What can I teach someone else about this book?*

A SUMMARY OF THE BENDS IN THE ROAD FOR THIS UNIT

Essential Question: Can I find a way for books to become my teachers, so that I can learn ideas and information about the world? Can books get me wondering about things?

- **Bend I: Readers Become Experts on Topics by Reading Books, Asking Questions, and Talking with Others**

  How can I notice more and more in the books I read?

- **Bend II: Readers Learn about Words inside Their Books, Too!**

  How can I learn new things and words from the pictures and words?

- **Bend III: Readers Can Think about What's the Same and What's Different in—and across—Books**

  If I put together a couple of books that are about one thing, how can I learn from one and add it to what I learn from the next?

In Bend I (Readers Become Experts on Topics by Reading Books, Asking Questions, and Talking with Others), you will launch students into the unit by telling them that reading is like an adventure! Readers go on trips in books and learn lots of information about the world. They go to zoos, parks, oceans, and more! Here, you will spend about a week and a half teaching readers how to study the topics their books are teaching them about, how to wonder and raise questions about the information, and how to study pictures and photographs to get more information about the topic of the book.

In Bend II (Readers Learn about Words inside Their Books, Too!), you will teach students to not only use the word-solving skills that they have been learning through the year but also to pay particular attention to parts of their books or words that seem important to the topic. You can teach students how to learn and think about domain-specific vocabulary they come across in their books. Plan to spend a little over a week in this bend.

In Bend III (Readers Can Think about What's the Same and What's Different in—and across—Books), you will teach kids how to think and talk about a topic across books. You may decide to gather two or more texts (perhaps even a basket) about the same topic and teach children how to reread books, finding and noticing things that are in both books and things that are decidedly *not* in both books—similarities and differences. It will take you about a week to wrap up the unit.

ASSESSMENT

As you gear up for this unit, you'll first want to find out what your readers already know about reading nonfiction. You might do an informal assessment during a read-aloud, selecting key points in an engaging high-interest text (one that is at grade-level text complexity) to pause and ask children to talk to one another. You can match your prompts to the key strategies and skills highlighted in this unit (questioning, word solving and vocabulary, comparing and contrasting). For example, in Bend I, you will be emphasizing questioning, so in your read-aloud assessment you might prompt students to share any questions they are thinking about with a partner. As children talk to one another, circulate around the room, making notes of their responses. You might be surprised at how difficult it can be for some children to generate questions. Do some children make statements about the text, rather than formulate questions? Do any children ask very obvious questions about the text, questions they clearly already know the answer to, and therefore aren't really authentic questions at all? As children talk, you can quickly ascertain who in your class will need support with this.

Perhaps you'll prompt children to figure out the meaning of key vocabulary since this is the major work of the second bend. You might stop at several words that are likely to be unfamiliar, and ask children to draw a picture representing what they think the word might mean, or to choose from three pictures the one that best matches the meaning. Then you can collect those pictures and quickly sort into rough groupings—children who had no difficulty figuring out the meaning of new vocabulary, children who showed some signs of understanding new vocabulary, and children who will clearly need lots of support with vocabulary.

As the unit unfolds, you might also do some assessment during conferring to see what children do when asked to compare and contrast information. Throughout the unit, you can check in with students using the books they are reading, or familiar read-alouds, asking questions such as, "Hmm, . . . It seems like baby rabbits are not that different from the baby squirrels we just learned about. What do you think? What's the same? What's different?" As you conduct this research as part of your regular conferring, you can jot notes that will help inform your teaching for the third bend in this unit. Look for patterns across your classroom: are kids able to see differences, but unable to see similarities where they exist? Do they perseverate on tiny details, missing the big picture?

You will also want to continue to use your running records to help you think about reading process and how your students are using and integrating the sources of information as they read. You will probably need to take running records to determine how your kids are approaching grade-level text complexity. Analyzing (formal or informal) running records will give you insight into the strategies your students rely on for decoding, fluency, and comprehension, as well as help you keep track of their progress up the gradient of book difficulty. Your analysis of their miscues will help you understand how they are integrating sources of information (meaning, syntax, and visual), and will also help you make decisions about what print work to teach each of your readers next. When you find a student stopping on a hard word in a fiction book and only using phonics to say it, often it is the case that she does the same in nonfiction books. You'll want to help such students set a goal to cross-check what they say and ask themselves, "Does that make sense?

Do I know a word that sounds similar that would match the information in the book?" This is an important goal in reading, regardless of the genre.

GETTING READY

Prepare your classroom library for nonfiction reading for beginning readers.

Your classroom library is an integral part of your reading workshop. It not only houses all the books—it is also the place where kids come to get inspired to read! Plan to arrange your library so that it's not simply a place for storing books. Your classroom library evolves and changes with your units, showcasing and displaying books that your students will want to read.

For this unit, you will probably want to arrange your classroom library so that it 1) supports young readers in finding books about topics they are interested in learning about, and 2) makes it easy for kids to find books that are within reach—books students can read independently—but still provides them with a slight challenge to encourage growth.

You might organize your classroom library into two halves: fiction on one side, and informational texts on the other. Then you can encourage kids to shop for informational books, while still having fiction books available as well. For this unit, a baggie full of informational texts is preferred, but students might add some fiction books to their baggie if supplies are low, or to meet a particular need or interest.

Within each half of your library, the baskets of books can be organized in various ways. You will probably want some baskets, perhaps a third of your library, organized by level, and others organized by topics, genre, or favorite authors. Setting up a portion of your library with leveled baskets on a mix of topics will make it quick and easy for kids to find just-right books.

In addition to baskets of leveled books, you can support children by organizing books (on both the informational and fiction sides of the library) into baskets based on topics (e.g., sports, ocean life, Star Wars, and pets), or favorite authors (such as Byron Barton, Lois Ehlert, or Todd Parr), or even series books (National Geographic Readers or DK Readers publish beautiful easy nonfiction series books). A large number of the books available at beginning reading levels tend to be concept books, so you may want to divide those into baskets as well: counting books, alphabet books, colors, shapes, and opposites, for example. If you are short on informational books, you might decide to create baskets that are a mix of fiction and informational books on one particular topic. In the third bend in particular, you'll be teaching students to fill their book baggies with books on a topic of interest, to support comparing and contrasting the information across books. Having a wide variety of books on hand, on common topics and interests, will be key.

Band together books on similar topics to support vocabulary development.

To support vocabulary, especially for students who are English language learners, you might go a step further and rubber-band together books on the same topic. For example, if you have a ton of books on farm animals, communities, and families in your level D basket, then you could band together all farm animal books, all community books, and so forth. During book shopping, then, guide your ELLs to select a stack of banded-together books so that when they read, they see the same content words repeated across several books.

Strategically assign partnerships for the unit.

Much of the work children do in this unit will be done with a partner. Children tend to have a lot to say about informational books, and a consistent reading partner will provide a supportive structure for children to ask questions, talk about their books, and use their expanding vocabulary. Reading partners can also support each other through the tricky parts. Partnerships that are based on reading level (homogeneous grouping) will have the advantage of being able to swap books at the end of the week, and read one another's books together throughout the week. However, even more important than swapping books is that reading partners work well together and can talk to one another. Occasionally you might decide to partner some students with a partner who reads a level or two up or down the ladder. In some special cases, you might decide to create a triad so that two students are productive, supportive partners, and are modeling that for a third student who is still learning the ways of reading partners.

In the third bend, children will be introduced to several reading games that they can play not just with their partner, but in groups at their desks or tables. You will want to be sure that your children are seated so that they can work alone, with their partner, and also with a group of four easily. It's helpful to seat kids so that there are two partnerships (or a partnership and a triad) sitting at each table or group. One routine is to have students sit at tables for reading time following the minilessons, but turn their chairs back-to-back with their reading partner during private reading time, then turn their chairs shoulder-to-shoulder during partner reading, then sit facing their whole table of four kids during any group work.

For this unit, you might decide to have kids work with partners immediately following the minilesson, and then settle into quiet, private reading time afterward. You may find that kids are excited about their informational books and have a lot to say, especially when initially choosing and starting a new book. Rather than fight it, capitalize on it by structuring the time for talk, followed by time to read.

Teach students how to select information books that are just right—not too easy, not too hard.

Before the first day of the unit, show students how you'd like them to shop for books. For this unit, you will want to encourage kids to find books that are both high interest and within reach. Show them how to browse the labels of the topic baskets, and how to shop through the baskets of leveled books as well. At the start of the unit, children might fill their book baggie with a variety of interesting topics (it isn't until later in the unit that you'll teach them to shop for books on just one topic). Together with their reading partner, they can ask, "Is this a book I might want to read?" Then teach them how to look at the covers and titles of the books to pull out books and give them a try. Emphasize choosing just-right books, books kids can read with 96 percent accuracy, strong comprehension, and fluency (with the exception of levels A–C, where you will provide a book introduction on a first read, and would expect "crisp" one-one pointing rather than fluency). If you find that some students are having difficulty selecting just-right texts from the unleveled

Readers Read With a Partner

Sit side-by-side.

Put one book in the middle.

See-saw read.

Share WOW! pages.

Reread to learn more.

Add a pinch of you.

portion of the library, you may decide to have them fill part of their baggie from the leveled section of the library, guiding them toward which baskets are good fits.

Children at beginning reading levels will need plenty to read. Usually about ten to twelve books in the book baggie will be the appropriate amount for the week, allowing for plenty of rereading. If you are short on books, you might decide to have each student choose some books from the fiction side of the library. You might decide to stretch the books you have by placing bins of informational books at tables and spots around the room for kids to share with partners or groups. You could divide your workshop time into informational reading time (following your minilesson), and then switch to fiction reading time, to help manage the amount of time children spend on each.

Make a plan for helping kids get to know the books available to them through a tour of the classroom library, book introductions, and more.

As children begin to select books, make sure that you are providing support whether they are reading levels A/B or F/G. At the beginning reading levels, children will rely on having a brief book introduction on the books that they choose from the classroom library. You might read the title, identify unfamiliar keywords or concepts, and have a brief conversation about the topic. If there is a pattern to the text, you might read the first line or two of the pattern they'll find on each page. You may make it a routine to read aloud a few pages of these little books each day, as a quick book introduction for the whole class, stopping after a page or so and saying, "I bet lots of you can't wait to have this book in your baggie!" You can also encourage same-level partnerships to swap some books at the end of each week—reading together, after all, is its own type of book introduction.

For children moving into levels D and E and above, a book introduction is highly supportive, but no longer as crucial. However, one of the most dramatic changes is that they will encounter more topics that are outside of their personal backgrounds. To support these children, you might encourage them to shop for more than one book on a topic so that they can read about one topic across several books, building important content vocabulary. This will also set them up well for the work of the final bend.

Gather informational texts to share during read-aloud and shared reading.

Read-aloud and shared reading will, as always, be a great time to explicitly model learning from books. In general, across the year you will probably want to make it a goal that nonfiction books and fiction are getting equal amounts of read-aloud time in your classroom. In this unit, you'll want to bring out your best, most beautiful information books for reading aloud and shared reading.

In Bend II, you will need a fresh informational big book to use for shared reading that contains domain-specific vocabulary. We mention *Zoo Looking* by Mem Fox, but you may want to select a book that ties in with your science or social studies curriculum. You will be creating a chart of vocabulary words from your shared reading text in Bend II, so it will be all the more meaningful and valuable if you create a chart students can use across the day. If you have already created vocabulary charts from other shared reading or read-aloud books, you may want to find them and refer to them during this unit.

Spruce up your libraries and pull out informational picture books and narrative books about similar topics from your baskets to use for read-alouds and shared reading. Place the books you select in full view—perhaps with covers facing out on top of your shelves and around your library—to entice your students with the array of topics they'll explore. Take out some informational big books and place them in a basket near the library. These will be great resources both for quick warm-ups before shared reading and for demonstrations during your minilessons.

BEND I: READERS BECOME EXPERTS ON TOPICS BY READING BOOKS, ASKING QUESTIONS, AND TALKING WITH OTHERS

Invite your students to learn about the world. Teach them that each new book they read helps them to become an expert on a topic.

In this first part of the unit, you will want to open the doors to learning about the world—through books! You will rally students' energy and enthusiasm to think about all the information there is to learn and talk about with one another, information that exists in books. You will want to help your readers not only to be excited about learning but also to develop and use their keen observational skills to learn more about and *question* what they see in books, to help them discover new things about the world. You might warm them up by saying something like, "Readers, you've been strengthening your reading muscles, getting better and better at learning to read. With each new book you read, you are learning new information, and new words, and new ideas. Did you know that the authors who wrote these books wrote them to teach you, so that you could become an expert, just like they are? Each new book adds to what you know, and before you know it, you're going to be experts, just like the authors who wrote these books." Then you might dramatically unveil the newly reorganized nonfiction section of your classroom library with great flourish, pulling back a piece of fabric that you've covered it in, or cutting a ribbon that has kept it closed off until now. "Hooray! It's nonfiction time!"

Perhaps you will launch this work by explaining to children that each book they are about to read is like taking a class from an expert on the topic. You might say something like, "Readers, this month we are going to work especially hard to not only read our books, but also learn from them as well. Readers look closely, and point to the pictures and ask questions, and talk about their books, so that they can become experts on the topics!"

From the start, teach students to use a whole repertoire of familiar strategies to read their books.

On this first day you might do a quick model of it all, inviting kids to show you what they can do, and linking this new work to familiar work.

> **"Today I want to teach you that reading nonfiction isn't all that different from reading fiction. Nonfiction readers use all the same strategies as fiction readers do when they are getting ready to read."**

In your minilesson, be sure to (briefly) model the getting-ready-to-read strategies you've already taught, using a big book or a book placed on a document camera, so that you and the kids can work together. Look at the cover, read the title, then walk through the pictures, naming what you see, and how you think the book will probably go. Think aloud about what you know about the topic that will help you read the book, and invite the kids to think along with you.

If you model with a book like *Who Works at the Zoo?* by Sarah Russell (published by National Geographic), you might say "Oh, I've been to a zoo before—so that makes me think this book will probably have many different animals in it." After previewing the text, turn to the first page and read the words: "'Many people work at the zoo.'" Say, "Hmm, . . . I know that a lot of people work at the zoo. Let's see . . . What questions does that make me think about?" Pause here and let the students think alongside you. You may say, "Does it make you think about any questions? I wonder, what kind of work do people do at the zoo? I think there are the people who feed the seals, and there are people who tell you where to go when you are lost. Maybe we will learn about them! Let me use my finger to point to the pictures, to help me learn more . . . Let's see . . . Here is the water. Oh! I have another question! Anyone else? I am wondering, 'What kind of animal may live here?' Was anyone else wondering that too? Let's read on to learn more and ask more questions!" After modeling, name what you just did so that your children can do it too. "Readers, did you see how we looked closely and pointed and asked questions to help us learn a lot from this page just like we did on our neighborhood walk? Let's do it again on the next page, and you all get ready to ask questions too!"

As the minilesson continues, engage children in trying the strategy themselves. Turn the page and let the children try learning a lot by looking closely, pointing, and asking questions. After children have tried this work during the active engagement, send them off to try it in their own books.

You will probably want to emphasize asking the kinds of questions that will help children focus on key details: Who? What? When? Where? How? Why? You may want to plan to model these often and regularly during your separate read-aloud time, so that when you demonstrate in a minilesson, children will already be quite familiar with posing these types of questions.

Teach students to talk about the information they are learning from any book—list books, concept books, pattern books, and nonfiction books.

While this unit focuses on learning from nonfiction books, it may be the case that children reading levels A–D will have books that are list books, concept books, or pattern books, and are not your typical nonfiction texts. Remember, they can learn from any book in their book baggie. Encourage readers to talk about what their books do teach, and help them to see how taking in the pictures and words can lead to questions and ideas that they can then ponder as they read the rest of the text. As kids read and explore the books in their book baggies, move about the class to research your readers to find out what skills seem to be in place already, and what some of the challenges are. Perhaps looking closely at the pictures was a snap, but no one in your class seemed to come up with questions as they read. Use this information to help you plan subsequent lessons or small-group work.

Across the first few days of the unit, help children to see what they have been missing in their books. Encourage them to move their finger across the page, noticing more and naming what they see. If children need more support with questioning, then you might teach them a few helpful question prompts such as: "I wonder why . . ." or "Where does . . . ?" or "What is this . . . ?" As soon as the questions start flowing—and they will—show children how they can use their talk time with partners to try to answer those questions. You will probably want to start a chart that lists some of these question starters, so that kids can continue to use it as a resource across the unit. In a minilesson you might start with just a few prompts, and then in the coming days and weeks during read-aloud, shared reading, and other minilessons you might add several more prompts.

> **"Today I want to teach you that when readers want to learn from their books they run their fingers across each page, trying to notice more and more in both the pictures and the words. As they do this they say what they notice and then ask questions about those details. They might ask, 'I wonder why . . .' or 'Where does . . . ?' or 'What is this . . . ?'"**

Emphasize that readers can teach each other new information, especially the main ideas and key details in their books.

Right from the start, foster the desire among readers to share what they have learned. Set up reading partnerships strategically so that students read at similar levels and can shop for books together, make book recommendations, and even swap books at the end of each week. If possible, pair kids with similar interests and strengths that complement one another. Perhaps one child may be very quiet, and another child is a great questioner and very patient. Perhaps two children have a shared interest in all things transportation: trains, planes, cars, trucks, and boats. You might start out partner work in this unit by teaching partners to read and retell together, taking turns retelling what the book was mostly about and giving examples. The listening partner can even add details the retelling partner forgot, or partners can reread their books together. Remind children of routines they probably already know by now: sitting shoulder-to-shoulder, or knee-to-knee, with one book in the middle as they read and talk together.

Teaching a partner about a book is a great way to practice naming the main topic or idea. Another strategy for teaching kids to talk and think about their books is to use the cover to name what the book is mostly about and reread the last page asking, "How does this ending go with all the pages and the title?"

> **"Readers, today I want to teach you that one way that expert nonfiction readers share what they are learning is by giving their partner a little lesson about their book. The lesson starts with looking at the cover and naming what the book is mostly about and then rereading the last page and asking 'How does this ending go with all the pages in the book and the title?'"**

This makes for a great conversation for reading partners—and many of their books will end with a page that sums up or fits with the main idea of the text. Some last pages might bring all the separate parts together (in a book that shows a different musical instrument on each page, it might end, "A band!"); other books might end with an invitation to the reader ("Now you try!"). In a share session, you can name some of the different ways that book endings might fit with the main idea.

Of course, some books will not have a last page that fits with the main idea. It is true that many information trade books provide one piece of information after another—and then they just end! You can teach kids to be on the lookout for those kinds of books, too, and when they find one, they might work together to create a new last page for the book—perhaps one that sums up the main idea, or brings all the information together, or invites the reader to do something. You might say, "Readers, I often find that I can't turn off the writing part of my brain! When I see an information book that just . . . ends . . . well, the writer in me just can't help it! I need to write an ending for it!" This will dovetail nicely with any of the information-writing units (*How-To Books: Writing to Teach Others* (Kindergarten, Unit 3), *Nonfiction Chapter Books* (Grade 1, Unit 2), or *Lab Reports and Science Books* (Grade 2, Unit 2). You might look at a few information books to notice some of the last pages, and gather ideas on a chart.

In your writing center or in a special basket located in the classroom library, you can provide special large Post-its® or squares of paper for doing this work, so that children can help themselves to these materials whenever they need them.

Perhaps you will also teach students to be reporters. They might hold microphones (toilet paper rolls with foam balls on top) and say, "This just in: Many things live near a pond. You can find ducks and spiders and turtles. They all live in the pond with the grass and the leaves!" While the children will be busy pretending to be reporters, you will help them to become clearer and clearer in naming what their books are mostly about.

Just as you taught children early in the bend to generate questions about a topic as they read, you might go on to teach that when readers talk with partners, they may be left with even more questions. Again, remind children that when they have questions they can talk about those questions with partners and look

Information Books Have Endings!

○ Some last pages sum up the main idea.

○ Some last pages bring all the separate information together on one page.

○ Some last pages invite the reader to do something.

○ Some last pages do all of those things and more!

to their books to do further thinking and learning. Teach them that readers can hold on to questions for a long time—as they continue to read new books and learn new things. In fact, sometimes they may come up with questions that linger for days, months, even years before coming across an answer or solution.

Assess your students' partner work by watching for how well they can talk back and forth about one topic. If children are simply waiting for their turn rather than actively talking back and forth, then you might teach them more ways to engage their partners while teaching. You can show them that pointing to pictures and words helps their partner to understand what they are teaching. You might also teach children to ask their partners questions as they teach and then look back through the book to answer them together.

Differentiate your instruction through small-group work and individual conferences.

Continue to pull small groups and introduce instructional-level texts to your readers. Some of your small-group work will likely help readers to ask questions. You might pull together a group of children who are still figuring out what a question is and read a text or two together, formulating and answering questions as you read. As the children become more comfortable with this work, you can have them work with partners as you coach them along.

Throughout the month, you will continue to gather small groups for both guided reading and shared reading. Here too, you might put an extra emphasis on helping children to look closely and learn from their books. Both shared reading and guided reading require students to reread texts in order to read with more automaticity, fluency, and comprehension. Because of the support of text introductions and the group, you will be able to put higher-level texts in children's hands, providing a text that is more complex, and allowing your readers to think deeply about what they are learning.

Remember that another big skill in this bend is understanding what your book is mostly about (which is different than listing all the key details). Take a look at running records, in addition to your conference notes, to determine who will need more support with this skill. You can pull a strategy group to teach children how reading the title and the last page can often help readers figure out what a book is mostly about. In the next part of this unit you will work more directly with vocabulary. Though, if some students would benefit from looking for and discussing newer words, then you might also start this small-group work during this bend.

BEND II: READERS LEARN ABOUT WORDS INSIDE THEIR BOOKS, TOO!

Begin the new bend in the road by highlighting domain-specific language—"expert words" that fit with a topic.

By now, your students are full of ideas about their books. When you listen to them talk, you hear them retell the main ideas from their books, and share questions they have about the information. However, they may not have gotten the hang of using new (and sometimes not-so-new) vocabulary and domain-specific language. Children might also continue to see each new piece of information as distinct and unconnected to the rest of the text. In this next portion of teaching (and learning), you will show students how to collect new vocabulary and facts as they read page after page, and then how to synthesize what they are learning. Readers will work hard to read new books, learn information from the words and pictures, seek out new vocabulary, and then talk about how all of these parts go together.

To launch this bend, you may want to create some excitement around learning new vocabulary by creating vocabulary charts to go along with your read-alouds and shared reading. During shared reading of *Zoo Looking* by Mem Fox, for example, you might ask kids to draw and label different animals on index cards, and then display them on a chart titled "Expert Zoo Words." Then, as you read other books about zoos, and encounter more vocabulary, you can add to the chart (e.g., *zookeeper, veterinarian, biologist*).

As a connection in your first minilesson of the bend, you might ask kids to search through their book baggies to see if they have any words that could be added to the chart. Then, with great excitement, you could announce to your class that they too can create their own "expert words" charts, to teach each other words from the books they have been reading.

> **"Today I want to teach you that one thing that expert nonfiction readers do is collect expert words about their topics—words that are important to know. They collect these words on a special chart and use them when they are teaching others."**

Distribute large sheets of paper so that students can create individual kid-sized word charts (legal size is probably big enough, but paper even larger than this will be a lot of fun for kids to use). As the workshop progresses, you might do a quick interruption to remind the class that picture clues will help them teach their partner the meaning of the vocabulary they've been recording, and they should also start a new chart for each new topic. For the next few share sessions, of course, you might select a few kid-created vocabulary charts to discuss as a class, adding more words, and then deciding on a place to display the vocabulary charts they've been creating (perhaps hanging sets of them on a clothesline, or making a whole book of charts to be kept in the classroom library).

As kids begin to read with a focus on important vocabulary, there are a couple of things that will happen as they read. One, readers will encounter important words, "expert words" that they know, familiar words that are important to the topic. Two, readers will encounter expert words that they *do not* know, that are important to the topic. You will want to support readers with both.

To start, you will probably want to talk to the class about rereading their books and finding important words that go with the topic of the book, and teach them that they can teach and report these words to their partners. Talk to them about how reporters do more than just report the word—they try and teach it! "Expert readers even use the pictures to teach the expert words. They can describe what it looks like or what the word does. Maybe they even give an example or two!"

This child made her own vocabulary chart based on her reading about pets. She listed key words from her reading that she could refer to when talking to a partner.

Secondly, you might say, "Readers, when you are reading to learn, you may come across words that you have never seen or heard before. For example, if you are reading a book about flowers, then there might be special words about flower parts in the book, like *stem* and *petals*, or if you are reading about animals playing together, then you may find words like *flap* and *gallop* to tell about how the animals move."

When children come across new vocabulary words like these, you will want them to use a whole repertoire of strategic actions to solve the word. First, they might use the pictures and the text to take a guess. "What would make sense?" they'll ask themselves. Then they'll try that word out in the sentence to see if it sounds right. If it does, they'll check the print more carefully to cross-check their original guess. They might check the first few letters, then the last few letters—often this is enough to figure out the word in a beginning leveled book. "Aha! My guess must be correct!" they'll say, and reread to smooth it out and continue on their way. Or, they'll say, "Whoops—that can't be it," and they'll take another guess. Eventually, they'll either figure out a word that makes sense, sounds right, and looks right—or they'll give it their best try and move on.

In this unit, you'll also want to highlight specific strategies to help them figure out the meaning of these domain-specific words. You might emphasize stopping at such words to ask, "What might this word mean? Are there any clues in the picture or in the other words on the page?"

In a minilesson, you could choose any informational leveled book to demonstrate. Perhaps you will choose a book like *Fishy Tales* from the DK Readers series. You might start on the first page, reading the text without difficulty, "Take a swim in the blue sea." Then you might say, "Hey wait a second! That word says 'sea' but it doesn't mean the same as, 'I can *see* you!' I'm a little confused. I'm going to need to do some work with this tricky word." Then you can go on to demonstrate how you can use the picture—it shows the ocean—and other words on the page—it says the sea is a place you swim *in*—to help you figure out what the word means. Let the children chime in as you look around the page, but be sure to show and tell them how *you* figure it out too!

As the lesson continues, you might have children practice the strategy on another page of *Fishy Tales*, or you might show them another book, so they can see the strategy transferred to another text. Either way, watch them during this active engagement to determine whether the entire class will need extra practice with this on another day, or perhaps a subset of the class, in a small group. As you send off your readers, be sure to remind them that they will be practicing all of their best reading strategies and that when they come to a word they are unsure of, they have this new strategy for figuring out what it means!

As the bend continues, teach students to synthesize information from both the pictures and the words.

As you move beyond vocabulary to teach students to synthesize the information in each book (pulling all the separate pieces of information together), it will be important to emphasize how partnerships can work together to study the pictures in their books. They may do this by pointing and labeling parts, commenting on what they see, and saying how parts of the picture go together. This heightens students' awareness of the big idea we hope to convey in this bend—that readers see *more* than just the text on the page. Of course, you'll also want to teach students that they need to fit the pictures and the words together. They need to use everything on the page—reading the pictures, then the words, then the picture again to understand everything on the page.

> **"Today I want to teach you that nonfiction readers use all of the information on the page to understand what they are reading. They don't just _collect_ words and facts and list them separately, like 'one, two, three.' No way! They work hard to pull all the separate pieces of information together. One way to do this is to point and label the separate parts of the picture and then say how the parts go together."**

As kids begin to look between the pictures and the words, thinking about how all the information fits together, teach them to "bring the book to life" by acting out the actions in the pictures and the words. They can match their voice and use gestures and actions to show what is happening. While using _Zoo Looking_ by Mem Fox in a minilesson, you can use gestures to show Flora looking at the animals, and then each animal doing a different action in response (the snake "slithers" for example). Model bringing the book to life by matching your voice and gestures to what is happening in the words and pictures on the page.

Remember to model learning from all kinds of books, including list and pattern books that are not so clearly informational. These kinds of books provide a great model for teaching children how readers use patterns in a book, or how the book tends to go, in order to get themselves ready to read every time they turn the page. Teach students that readers think about the pattern the text is following as well as what the book is about in order to figure out tricky words. For example, after reading a few pages of _Eating the Alphabet_ by Lois Ehlert you can look more closely at a picture and ask, "What do I expect these words to say (even if some of the words are too hard to read)?" Model using the letter of the alphabet as a clue, and also the pattern the book has been following, as you try to word solve. Think aloud, saying, "Well, I know that it has to be a food because the whole book is about food! I can't very well say 'truck,' right?" This will help children to not only process what the print of this particular page says, but also to think about how the pages fit together. You might reread and notice, "Wait, it's not just any old food—it's all fruits and vegetables!"

You might ramp up this work for partnerships by teaching them more advanced ways of inspecting photographs and pictures together. One way to do this is to demonstrate how you can read a page and then talk about how the picture on the page helped you to add on to the information you gathered from the text. For instance, if the print says, "Monkeys climb trees" and the photograph paired with that text depicts a monkey hanging from a tree limb with just one hand, then you could talk about how even though the _words_ just teach the reader that monkeys climb trees, the _picture_ teaches the reader that monkeys have strong arms that help them as they climb and hang from trees. Teach students to respond to the text by saying things like, "The words say _____. I also see _____ in the picture, and it makes me think _____." That is, you will ask children to "apply concepts," which is higher-level thinking than simply retelling.

You'll probably want to wrap up this bend with a repertoire lesson that revisits some of the strategies you previously taught—especially reminding children to read in ways that help them figure out what each book is mostly about. You might use a chart as a visual reminder of several key strategies, and then demonstrate pausing on each page to think, "How does this fit with the title? . . . Now how does *this* fit with the title?" You also want to stop midway to think, "How do all these pages fit together so far?" and again to think, "What is this *whole* book mostly about?" This work will set children up to understand and remember information more easily. Synthesizing information and summarizing topics and main ideas, rather than trying to hold on to every fact, will serve them well as readers.

> **"Readers, I want to remind you that readers don't usually try to memorize every tiny fact in their books! Rather, they use strategies to figure out what the book is mostly about. As they read, they are thinking, 'How does this page fit with the title? . . . Now how does *this* page fit with the title?' They also stop midway to think, 'How do all these pages fit together so far?' And again to think, 'What is the *whole* book mostly about?' Readers are doing a lot of stopping and thinking all along the way to figure out what the book is mostly about."**

Differentiate your vocabulary instruction through small-group work.

This is a good time to imagine vocabulary-rich small-group work that supports readers working with books at a high level of text complexity, as they practice decoding and using meaning to understand more challenging texts. You might gather a group of readers who read at the same level, and select copies of books that are at children's instructional levels to do some guided reading or shared reading with a focus on vocabulary.

Before reading, select a few vocabulary words. Think about selecting words that might be difficult for children to read but are important to know. The selected words should help students make sense of the text. These could even be domain-specific vocabulary. You might start the small group by saying, "Readers, we are going to read a really interesting book today—one that will teach us a lot! But before we read it, I want to show you some of the very important expert words that you will find in the book." Show the words to the children and allow them to figure out each one with the help of a partner, while providing them with the necessary support. Then, invite the children to think about the sentences that could appear in a book containing these words. You might say, "Hmm, . . . We know the word *butterfly* is going to be in this book—what do you think a sentence in the book, using this word, will sound like?" Once the children have thought of some plausible sentences, you can do small-group shared reading or have the students partner read. Following the first reading, work with the students to pose questions and then have them reread to practice reading more independently and more fluently.

You may also want to incorporate some word work into your conferring and small groups. As children encounter unfamiliar vocabulary, they will certainly need to draw on all they can to solve the word, figure out how pronounce it, and then attach meaning to the new word. In levels A–D, your readers will need practice and support with using the picture to take a guess and then looking to the first letter (or first few letters) to double-check their guesses. Toward levels C/D, you'll want to coach students to also look to the last few letters as a way to cross-check their guess.

In level E, as well as F/G, your readers may need some help with breaking words apart into familiar spelling patterns, rather than trying to read letter by letter. As part of a book introduction in a guided reading lesson, you might select a few unfamiliar vocabulary words to work on. Write one on a small white board, and ask the kids to do the same. Then invite them to draw lines to show how they would break the word apart into parts. Kids can then compare the various ways they broke the word apart. For example, the word *slither* could be broken in several ways: sl/i/th/er, slith/er, sl/ith/er, and so on. The important takeaway is not that there is a "correct" way to break a word apart; rather, it is that when they encounter a new word, they can try multiple ways to work on it, using familiar spelling patterns, or parts of words. As children learn more and more about how syllables work during word study time, you can incorporate open- and closed-syllable lessons as an option for how to solve an unfamiliar word (/slith/ is a closed syllable, so we know the "i" must be a short vowel sound, which helps us to pronounce the word).

Of course, any word solving you teach needs to begin and end with meaning, so you'll continue to return to emphasizing that kids figure out how to say the word—but then always, *always*, try and figure out what it probably means. You might teach readers that if they are really stumped by a word, they should try everything they can, and then mark it with a Post-it to talk about with a partner.

BEND III: READERS CAN THINK ABOUT WHAT'S THE SAME AND WHAT'S DIFFERENT IN (AND ACROSS) BOOKS

Be sure each student has access to multiple books on a topic. Teach children to read and talk about information from across texts.

In this final part of the unit, you will teach children two big things: how to combine their learning from more than one book, and how to compare and contrast books. Looking across books in this way opens up multiple perspectives to our students, allowing them to look for commonalities and differences across the information they are gaining as they read.

To launch this bend, you will first need to be sure that your students have several books on the same topic. You might decide to plant these books in their book baggies and let them "discover" them there. Alternatively, you might let the children know during their book-shopping time that this week they will need to select some books that go together. Then, you can guide them as they choose. Another option might be to make bins of books that cluster around a topic, and then let children share books from these topic bins. If you do this, then remember that the bins will need to match the level of the readers who are reading from them.

In your first minilesson of the bend, engage the children in the new and exciting work of looking at books side by side. You might say, "When readers are learning about a new topic and becoming experts on that topic, they read *everything* they can! They read and read and read, trying to say everything they learned about that topic from all the books!" Invite your children to read their books and then try to say as much as they can about a topic. You might even encourage partners to count how many things they can say about a topic after reading one book, and then count again after reading a second book. The goal here is for the children to get excited about learning and saying more after reading more books.

On this first day, many children will start to remember other books they have read that go with their topics, too. You can encourage them to find those books and add them to their collection. This sort of agency is important in learning, and when it blossoms, you will want to feed it!

As this bend continues, teach partnerships to compare and contrast within one book and across books.

Once your children are excited to collect lots of information from across books, you can move them into some more advanced work. You might teach partnerships to compare and contrast by teaching them to play the "Same Game."

> **"Today I want to teach you that readers compare books, noticing what is the same and also what is different. You can do this by playing the Same Game and the Different Game."**

Explain to the class how they could play this game with their partners. "You can turn the pages of your book and think, 'What's the same?' on each page. Then, you can put a Post-it on pages that are the same, and write 'S' so that you can share this with your partner." Once kids are able to talk with a lens toward similarities you can teach them to think, "What's different?" and put a Post-it labeled "D" on these pages, to share with a partner. Partners can play the "Different Game," as they notice differences across their books. They might say things like, "Our books are both about _____ but the pages are different. My pages go like _____ and yours go like _____." To get even more reading mileage out of this partner game, you can teach students to reread lines and even whole parts to each other as they talk about the information they have learned. Kids might take turns reading lines or parts together.

Across this series of lessons, you'll help children dig deeper into compare-and-contrast work. You might teach your most sophisticated readers to think about what the author of each book is trying to teach. Remind children that the teaching that is done through pictures and the teaching that is done through words may either be the same or be different. Using a page or two from a nonfiction shared reading experience, you might show students how to say, "The picture teaches me _____, but/and the words on this page say _____."

Readers Compare and Contrast Books

Next, you might teach readers to play a variation on the Same Game/Different Game at their tables, as small groups, called "Does Your Book Have . . . ?" This game will support work around craft and structure. One child chooses a book, or a page in a book and says what it's mostly about, then says, "Does your book have a text feature like this?" For example, the child might share a table of contents, or a glossary, or a caption to a photograph. Then the other three children search their books to see if they have a similar feature in their books. When they find something, they hold it up and share it with their group to say how it is similar (or different). This often involves discussing the purpose of the feature. "My table of contents is similar to yours because it is at the start of the book and it names all the chapters." Then it starts again; the other three children search to see if they can find a text feature that is similar to the latest page or book that was shared. (Don't be surprised to find that the whole group spends a good chunk of partner time rereading all the books in their baggies, searching for something to share, paying particular attention to the text features—that is the point!)

As children share parts of their books, comparing pages and talking about how parts are similar and different, they'll invent their own engaging ways to talk about their books. They might decide to act parts out, or read an entire (short) book to their group, or ask a question to the group. Kids will enjoy the new structure of being in small groups rather than partnerships, and by being in groups, this will increase the chances that they'll find meaningful connections across books. Surely someone, out of the four of them, will find a connection.

> "Today I want to teach you that you can invent your own ways to talk about books with your group. You might decide to act parts out, or read an entire (short) book to your group, or ask a question to the group. Work together to keep your conversations going. It's up to you!"

You can also show partners how to talk across books by asking, "What did the authors want us to learn about this topic? Let's look at what is the same and what is different about the information on the pages." This way, you set children up to look across the texts and begin to notice things that will help them as they carry on in their own books. Your students will be inferring and synthesizing information as they engage with comparing and contrasting across their books.

In all of this work, students have been considering what different books and authors can teach about the same topics. Depending on your library, those topics might be broader or more focused. If the books for this unit come only from your own classroom library, then you may find that your topics are broad ones such as animals, places, and family. If, however, you can combine libraries with your colleagues, then you might have more focused topics such as insects and mammals, cities and countries, or siblings and parents. Teach your readers to lay books side by side and then ask themselves, "What did I learn about the topic from this one, and what did I learn about it from this other one?"

> **"Readers can lay books side by side and then ask themselves, 'What did I learn about the topic from this one and what did I learn about it from this other one?'"**

Essentially, you'll be teaching kids that it is important to listen to many voices to learn. Layering multiple thoughts and perspectives allows you to say more about a topic. After reading several books on a single topic, your kindergarten students can meet with their partners to share all that they are learning. They can move from book to book, saying a sentence or two about the learning that they did in each one.

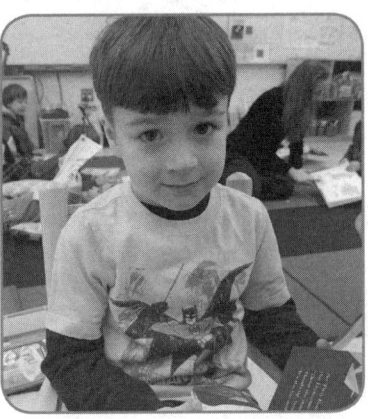

CELEBRATION

As this unit comes to an end, your children can celebrate all that they have learned about themselves and their world by making public the most interesting things that they have learned from their books. Each child can pick one or two books they love and write a statement—on sentence strips—about something they learned from reading, then tuck the strip inside the book in preparation for the celebration. During interactive writing, create a heading with the class for the outside bulletin board, letting the children help compose the wording. An example of this might be, "We Are Experts on Many Topics!" Then, gather the children to help create a reading bulletin board in the hallway. Ask each child to come up and share their book, saying something like, "This book is called *Owls*, and it taught me that owls can't turn their eyes; they have to turn their whole head to see what's around them!" Then, the book is ceremoniously clipped and hung up with a pushpin along with the child's sentence strip. Once every book and strip is hung up, have a big round of applause for the now older and wiser students standing in front of you!

POSSIBLE TEACHING POINTS

BEND I: READERS BECOME EXPERTS ON TOPICS BY READING BOOKS, ASKING QUESTIONS, AND TALKING WITH OTHERS

- "With each new book you read, you are learning new information, and new words, and new ideas. Each new book is like taking a class from an expert. This month we are going to work especially hard, to not only read our books but also to learn from them. Today I want to teach you that readers look closely, point to the pictures, ask questions, and talk about their books, so that they can become experts on the topics!"

- "Today I want to teach you that reading nonfiction isn't all that different from reading fiction. Nonfiction readers use all the same strategies as fiction readers do when they are getting ready to read."

Use this list as a menu of possibilities, selecting only the teaching points that meet the needs of your students. Use your assessment data (running records, conferring and small-group notes, observations, responses to read-alouds, and other information) to decide on a plan that is tailored to the needs of your class. These teaching points may be used as whole-class minilessons, mid-workshop teaching, or for conferences and small-group work. You need not use every teaching point. See the unit overview for guidelines on how much time to spend in each bend.

- "Today, I want to teach you that readers use the whole page and their whole brain to learn as much as possible about their books. They look closely at the entire page, and point and talk about everything they see—and most of all, readers ask questions."
    - Readers especially think and wonder about key details: Who? What? When? Where? How? Why?"
- "Today, I want to teach you that when readers want to learn from their books they run their fingers across each page, trying to notice more and more, in both the pictures and the words. As they do this they say what they notice and then ask questions about those details. They might ask, 'I wonder why . . .' or "Where does . . . ?' or 'What is this . . . ?'"
- "Readers, now that you've been learning so much from your books, you are ready to be the teachers! One way to teach your partner what you have learned is to do a retelling. One partner can say what the book was mostly about, and then give examples. Say, 'This book was mostly about _____. One example was _____.'
    - Your partner can even help you remember any important examples you might have forgotten.
    - You and your partner can reread your book to remember what it was mostly about and to search for examples."
- "Readers, today I want to teach you that one way that expert nonfiction readers share what they are learning is by giving their partner a little lesson about their book. The lesson starts with looking at the cover and naming what the book is mostly about and then rereading the last page and asking 'How does this ending go with all the pages in the book and the title?'"
- "Readers, today I want to teach you a little secret about some of your information books: some of your books do not have a last page that fits with the main idea! It is true that many information books provide one piece of information after another—and then they just end! You can be on the lookout for those kinds of books, and when you find one, you can get paper and create a new last page for the book.
    - Some last pages sum up the main topic. ('Animals live at the zoo.')
    - Some last pages bring all the separate information together on one page. ('Monkey, zebra, giraffe, lion, and hippo are all here together!')
    - Some last pages invite the reader to do something. ('Now go visit a zoo!')
    - Some last pages do all of those things and more!"
- "Readers can also be like television reporters, to teach others about the information they have been gathering. Reporters say things like, 'Did you know . . . ? Another interesting piece of information is . . . In this book it teaches you all about . . .'
    - Reporters often use gestures to add to their meaning.
    - Reporters can also point to the part of the book that fits with what they are saying."

- "Readers, you already know that you can come up with questions about a topic as you read, and today I want to teach you that you might *also* come up with questions about a topic when talking with your partners. Sometimes, after listening to your partner, you might be left with even more questions! You can ask your partner questions, and then work together to think of possible answers.
  - You and your partner might reread a book to search for answers.
  - As you talk, you might point to pictures and words to make sure you both understand what is being said.
  - You and your partner might search for new books the next time it's your turn to book-shop to help answer your questions.
  - Sometimes you have to hang on to a question for a long time before you find an answer: days, weeks, even years!"

BEND II: READERS LEARN ABOUT WORDS INSIDE THEIR BOOKS, TOO!

- "Today I want to teach you that one thing expert nonfiction readers do is collect expert words about their topics—words that are important to know. They collect these words on a special chart and use them when they are teaching others."

- "Today I want to tell you that not only do your books teach *you* important words—your *partner* can learn those words, too, and you can teach them! When you teach your partner the important 'expert words' in your book, you can do more than just say the words. You can use the pictures to teach an expert word. You can describe what it looks like or what the word does. You can even give an example or two to go with the word."

- "Readers, when you are reading to learn, you may come across words that you have never seen or heard before. For example, if you are reading a book about flowers, then there might be special words about flower parts in the book like *stem* and *petals*, or if you are reading about animals playing together, then you may find words like *flap* and *gallop* to tell about how the animals move. When you come to tricky words like this, you can stop and think, "What might this word mean? Are there any clues in the picture or in the other words on the page?
  - Readers ask themselves what word would make sense and try it out to see if it sounds right.
  - Readers check the print carefully, looking at the first few letters and also maybe at the end of the word."

- "Today I want to teach you that nonfiction readers use all of the information on the page to understand what they are reading. They don't *just* collect words and facts and list them separately, like 'one, two, three.' No way! They work hard to pull all the separate pieces of information together. One way to do this is to point and label the separate parts of the picture and then say how the parts go together."

- "Today I want to teach you that readers can 'bring the book to life' by acting out the actions in the pictures, and in the words. You can match your voice to what is happening, and use gestures and actions to add to what is happening."

- "Today I want to teach you that readers can get themselves ready to read every time they turn the page by thinking about what pattern the text is following and what the book is about. You can look closely looking at the picture and think, 'What is this page teaching? What might this page say?' Then, you can read to make sure the words match!"

- "Readers can respond to the text by reading the words and then using the pictures to learn even more information. They say things like, 'The words say _____. I also see _____ in the picture and it makes me think _____.'"

- "Readers, I want to remind you that readers don't usually try to memorize every tiny fact in their books! Rather, they use strategies to figure out what the book is mostly about. As they read, they are thinking, 'How does this page fit with the title? . . . Now how does *this* page fit with the title?' They also stop midway to think, 'How do all these pages fit together so far?' and again to think, 'What is this *whole* book mostly about?' Readers are doing a lot of stopping and thinking all along the way to figure out what the book is mainly about."

BEND III: READERS CAN THINK ABOUT WHAT'S THE SAME AND WHAT'S DIFFERENT IN (AND ACROSS) BOOKS

- "Today I want to teach you that when readers are learning about something, they read *everything* they can about the topic. They read more than one book about it! You can read many books about your topic and then retell everything you learned."

- "Today I want to teach you that readers compare books, noticing what is the same and also what is different. You can do this by playing the Same Game and the Different Game."

- "Readers, today I'd like to teach you that you can use both the pictures and the words to think about what's the same, and what's different. Sometimes the words are the same as what is in the picture, but sometimes they're different! As you read, to your partner or yourself, you can think and say, 'The picture teaches me _____, but/and the words on this page say _____.'"

- "Today I want to teach you that nonfiction readers notice text features as they are reading. You can do this with your partner by playing a game called, 'Does Your Book Have . . . ?' One reader chooses a book or a page in a book and says what it's mostly about, and then says, 'Does your book have a text feature like this?' Then the other kids at your table search their books to see if they have a page that has a text feature similar to the one you just pointed out. When they find something, they hold it up, share it with the group, and talk about what the purpose of the text feature is. Then it starts again!"

1. Say what the page or whole book was mostly about.

2. Ask, 'Does your book have a text feature like this?'

3. Everyone searches to see if they have a similar text feature.

4. When one person finds something, they share it with the group.

5. Start again!"

- "Today I want to teach you that you can invent your own ways to talk about books with your group. You might decide to act parts out, or read an entire (short) book to your group, or ask a question to the group. Work together to keep your conversations going. It's up to you!"

- "Today I want to teach you that readers can think about everything that authors want them to learn about a topic. They can compare different books on the same topic and ask themselves and each other, 'What did the authors want us to learn about this topic?' Readers look at what is the same and what is different about the information on the pages. Then they can reread to find parts that are similar and different across books."

- "Readers can lay books side by side and then ask themselves, 'What did I learn about the topic from this one and what did I learn about it from this other one?'"

Readers Are Resourceful

Tackling Hard Words and Tricky Parts in Books

RATIONALE/INTRODUCTION

Watch children playing in a sandbox, and you will see problem solving at its finest. A child begins to scoop away at the sand little by little with a spoon, then realizes there's a better tool, a spade, that will get the job done more quickly. Another child fills a pail with sand only to find that the sand is stuck when she tips it over to dump it out. What does she do? Does she give up? Of course not! She whacks the bottom of the pail until the sand pops out. When children reach for materials and tools in creative ways to solve problems, they are doing just what readers need to do—they are being resourceful. Rather than give up, they tackle tricky situations, using every trick and tool they can think of.

This unit highlights foundational skills for beginning readers, especially readers who are reading at or near levels C, D, and E. Of course, in every unit you've been featuring strategies for solving words in your instruction. This is a unit that will be just right for children who are beginning to put it all together: using directionality, searching for meaning in the pictures, having word-by-word matching, recognizing sight words in the context of reading, holding onto the patterns in their texts, and using these as a support when they read.

If your students are kindergartners and could use some repeated practice with the print strategies you taught in *Bigger Books, Bigger Reading Muscles* (Unit 3), then you might teach this unit to extend that work. You might pull certain bends from this unit and insert them into *Bigger Books, Bigger Reading Muscles* as extensions. Another option might be to teach this unit sometime after, as a chance for repeated practice.

You might consider this unit for first-graders, if your students need more support with print strategies after the first unit of study and are mostly reading levels C/D/E. If that is the case, you may want to teach this unit following *Building Good Reading Habits* (Unit 1), and before diving into *Learning About the World: Reading Nonfiction* (Unit 2).

This unit is designed both to teach children more strategies for word solving, cross-checking, self-correcting, and meaning making, and to model for them the resiliency of careful readers. We want children to know that careful readers don't give up, pass over, or ignore hard parts in their books.

ASSESSMENT

As you plan instruction for this unit, think about the strategy needs your children have by looking at assessment data and the corresponding analysis to see what they are doing as they read, so you can determine the necessary next steps. You'll want to be conducting running records on a routine basis to stay on top of children's ever-changing reading levels and evolving reading behaviors and habits.

You'll need to investigate children's current independent and instructional levels, as well as levels that are hard (sometimes referred to the child's "frustration" levels or ceiling) to determine what strategies they will need to read the next levels with proficiency. If you study a running record with very few miscues, it won't provide very much information about what the child struggles with! Look for patterns in each child's reading to help you set goals for individuals, and for your whole class.

Many teachers find it helps to have ready a whole-class list while conducting running records so they can jot down goals for each one of the children as they go. A list of instructional goals for your class might include "self-monitoring," "previewing the text, making predictions, and checking them," "using visual information to cross-check," or "using meaning to make a guess that makes sense." Your decisions about goals for each child will be based on your knowledge of the reading process and children's development as readers (you can refer to the *A Guide to the Reading Workshop, Primary Grades* section on this), including accuracy, fluency, and comprehension.

In addition, you might want to look closely at students' spelling assessment data, to consider what to teach during the word-study portion of your day. You can then help children use what they know about spelling to problem solve tricky words on the run in their reading. It will be helpful to know which exact spelling patterns your children have mastered so that you can refer, with specificity, to the tools they can use for figuring out words.

This will also be an important time to assess high-frequency word knowledge. Children who struggle in the early levels of reading often have a somewhat low high-frequency word vocabulary. Use the various formative assessments to collect data throughout this unit, to address your students' needs, and to move them as readers. If you find that some of your students know fewer words by sight, you can provide support for this in small groups as well.

You might also want to take a look at children's on-demand writing for insight into how children are handling challenging words. Children who are writing with a vowel sound for each word, have a growing bank of high-frequency words they can spell automatically, and can write complete sentences are demonstrating not only knowledge about conventions in writing—this also reveals quite a bit about what they will understand as readers and the knowledge about letters and words they might be able to draw upon when they come to tricky words in books. Children who are writing longer sentences, with approximated spellings that are closer and closer to conventional spelling (within-word pattern, or syllables and affixes stages) will likely be ready for more challenging books as readers.

A SUMMARY OF THE BENDS IN THE ROAD FOR THIS UNIT

Essential Questions: How can I be strong when I get to the hard parts in books so that I don't give up? Can I use strategies I know when books get hard?

- **Bend I: Readers Think about the Story and How the Book Sounds to Figure Out Words**

  How can I think about the story and about how books sound to help me figure out tricky words?

- **Bend II: Readers Are Flexible Problem Solvers**

  How do I make sure I notice when something I read doesn't make sense or sound right and then use multiple strategies to fix up my reading?

- **Bend III: Readers Make Their Reading Sound Great!**

  How can I reread my books many times to make my reading sound better and to help me understand more about the books?

In Bend I (Readers Think about the Story and How the Book Sounds to Figure Out Words), you'll invite students to be resourceful problem solvers, using all that they can to solve words. Many readers may tend to rely on the print when it comes to solving unfamiliar words (i.e., they rely on visual cues). This bend aims to extend students' word-solving strategies to include meaning cues and syntax/structure cues. You may need to spend a little over a week working in this bend.

In Bend II (Readers Are Flexible Problem Solvers), students will learn additional strategies for figuring out tricky words while learning to be flexible and transfer strategies from one tricky word to the next and across texts. You'll teach students that flexible readers don't just try one strategy and give up—they give it their best, making multiple attempts to solve those tricky words. Plan to spend a little over a week in Bend II.

In Bend III (Readers Make Their Reading Sound Great!), students will spend about a week learning many ways to reread. You'll teach them that readers in real life reread for many purposes—to solve tricky words, to notice new things in their books, and to smooth out their reading. They will, independently and in partnerships, make plans for rereading as they move from book to book.

GETTING READY

Prepare your classroom library and teach children how they need to shop for books in this unit.

In this unit students may read a mix of fiction, nonfiction, and other text types of leveled text, such as pattern books or rhyming books. As is the case in many units, you'll want to arrange your classroom library with a section containing baskets of books organized by levels, while the rest of the library may be organized into baskets of authors, topics, text types, and series. You may want to divide your library into two general parts: informational books and fiction. You can then encourage kids to select some books from both.

Children reading at the beginning levels that this unit is targeted toward will be reading books that are only a few pages long. They will need plenty of books in their book baggies to keep them focused and engaged. Remind children how to do a quick preview of each book to decide if the book is one they want to keep for the week. Ten to twelve books are usually the appropriate number of just-right books for students at levels A–G to last them for the week. This allows for ample opportunity for rereading (important for learning new vocabulary, high-frequency words, fluency, repeated practice with applying strategies, and more). You'll also want each student to have several more challenging books in their book baggie. You'll need to plan to provide support (especially by way of book introductions) for those books at instructional level texts.

Make the most of reading partners by pairing students strategically and coaching into their work together.

Although we often pair readers homogeneously, at similar reading levels, so that they can share leveled books, you may opt to place students who are in transition between levels in a level-up partnership. For example, you may want your children who read levels A/B in a partnership with a solid C reader. When such partnerships meet, they will read C level books chorally or the A/B reader will echo his or her partner. This helps the child who reads levels A/B negotiate the challenges of the level C book with support. You may also decide to pair kids who are moving into D and E leveled texts in similar ways, to give them that boost up to the next level.

Partner reading also exposes kids to new books, providing a type of book introduction so that children may shop for books that they have read together with a level-up partner. Children could also swap books and make recommendations to each other. To manage the time, you may want to structure your workshop so that you begin every day with a brief minilesson at your classroom meeting area, followed by private reading time, where children might spread out throughout the room, sitting back-to-back with their reading partner. After an extended amount of private reading time, you'll signal to your children that it is time for partner reading, at which point they can turn their chairs shoulder-to-shoulder and sit together with one book in the middle. Finally, you'll wrap up your workshop with a share, either back at the classroom meeting area, or occasionally with children sitting at their reading spots with partners. A consistent structure for the unit will allow children to get the hang of the routine, so that they can concentrate on their books and what their partner has to say, rather than wondering where to go or what's coming next.

Display relevant charts and tools from previous units, and plan to create new anchor charts.

You may want to bring out any charts you may have created from previous units that relate to word solving so that children can build on previous learning. There will be times when you may want to teach minilessons that invite children to draw from the old charts and apply those strategies to the books they are reading now.

You might decide to make small copies of those charts so that students can have them up close. Perhaps you'll make copies to slip into a sheet protector inside a folder of reading resources, or perhaps you'll shrink them down to the size of an index card, so that kids can have a ring of mini-charts by their sides as they read. Some teachers put mini-charts on display at the center of each table on a flip chart, or in a plastic menu holder, making those familiar charts easily accessible.

Plan for new charts as well. Perhaps you will want to designate an area of your classroom where all the reading workshop charts will go, so that children know exactly where to look to find support for reading.

Gather books to use for read-aloud and shared reading.

In this unit, your students will be reading a mix of fiction and nonfiction, so you will probably want to make an extra effort to divide your read-alouds between both. Across the school year you will want to be sure that nonfiction books and fiction are getting equal amounts of read-aloud time in your classroom. As you read aloud informational books, you'll want to think aloud and model how readers think about main ideas and key details as they read and learn about informational topics. You can invite kids to discuss the information, discussing the big ideas and topics they learned and sharing their thoughts about the books.

As you read aloud fiction, you'll want to highlight thinking about what is happening in the book, keeping track of events by retelling often, and rereading when things are getting confusing. You'll want to think aloud about the characters' actions and words, and how those are clues to help us figure out how the character might be feeling. Invite children to have conversations about the story, including how the character feels about key events in it.

You can use shared reading as an opportunity for children to orchestrate all the strategies they will be learning across this unit. In minilessons, they will be introduced to one strategy at a time; in shared reading they can practice several strategies at once. For example, in one shared reading session you might encourage children to preview the text, make a prediction about what will happen, read from the beginning with expression, pause to check the picture to solve a tricky word, read on to figure out what a new word might mean, reread to put it all together, and finally revise the prediction that they originally made. You will probably want to select big books (or leveled books to use on a document camera) that lend themselves to word solving—choose a book that is two or three levels higher than the bulk of your class so that there will be plenty of challenge. Remember, you'll be rereading the book many times and providing significant scaffolding and support.

BEND I: READERS THINK ABOUT THE STORY AND HOW THE BOOK SOUNDS TO FIGURE OUT WORDS

Launch the unit by drawing a connection between being resourceful and solving problems in life—to being a resourceful problem solver as a reader.

As you launch this unit, you may recall examples of times when your students have been resourceful problem solvers. Think back on times when your class solved a problem or overcame a challenge. You might also remind students of familiar stories where characters solved a problem. Invite students to think and talk about what makes someone a great problem solver: someone who never gives up, a person who works together with other people, someone who uses everything he or she can to figure things out. Perhaps you'll create a chart that lists some of the ideas kids share about what makes someone a resourceful problem solver, or perhaps you'll give kids a moment to draw a picture of a time they solved a problem. Let children know how proud you are that they are becoming the kind of students who never give up—in fact, when the going gets tough, they just get going!

You will want to let your children know that just like there are problems in life that need solving, readers need to be resourceful problem solvers to understand their books. Because this unit is geared toward students reading levels C, D, and E, using meaning, syntax/structure, and visual/graphophonics (MSV) to solve words will be an important focus. Children will be learning that readers cross-check readily and fix up their mistakes quickly, in order to hold on to the greater meaning of the text. Before teaching this unit, you may find that many of your students are relying heavily on the visual/graphophonic sources of information (i.e., the print) while not fully grasping or using meaning and syntax (i.e., the pictures and the story, plus the patterns and sentence structure). This bend will teach students what it means to read for meaning and how to cross-check.

Teach an inquiry lesson to introduce the work of the unit.

You could launch this unit with a guided inquiry. "Readers," you might start, "I have been so impressed with your work in the last few months. You are reading harder books, reading more books, and reading for longer amounts of time. You are really getting better and better, and stronger and stronger! I even notice that more of you look at the words in your books and say things like, 'Hey, I know that word . . . and that word too!' I see you pointing to words in your books and helping your partners realize how many words you know in a snap! Give yourselves a pat on the back!

"But I have a question for you. How do you know when things aren't making sense? How do you know when you might need to go back and fix up your reading?" Pause to allow students to turn and talk, and then invite them to watch you as you read.

> **"Today we are going to investigate the question, 'How do readers know when they need to go back and fix things up? What are the signs to be on the lookout for?'"**

Invite students to watch you as you read. "See if you can tell when I need to go back and fix up my reading." As you read, demonstrate a number of obvious telltale signs that you need to apply some fix-up strategies. Pause after each mishap, saying, "Thumbs up if you think I should go back to fix up my reading." As kids notice your mishaps, you might keep a running list:

Readers watch out for signs to go back and fix things up:

- mumbling
- saying a word that doesn't make sense
- saying a word that definitely doesn't sound right in the sentence
- saying all sounds—not a word
- not able to retell

After modeling just a few of these, ask your kids to turn and talk one last time, "How do you know when you need to go back to fix things up?" Then end your minilesson with a reminder to give tricky words and tricky parts their very best guess, and then move on. This inquiry is designed to teach your students to self-monitor as they read. After all, how can they work hard on tricky words if they aren't even realizing which parts are tricky?

In a minilesson, demonstrate how readers don't just focus on the print—they also use the meaning of the story to figure out tricky parts.

When it clicks for new readers and they realize that they really *know* that the word on the page spelled t-h-e is "the," everything changes. The excitement of *really* reading can be overwhelming. Many students are so taken by this feeling that they forget to use what they know about the story and about books to help them read. They try to read each word using only the black marks on the page, and then their reading falls apart. The goal, then, is to help children integrate all sources of information (meaning, structure, and visual/graphophonics), but first you will need to be sure they understand what it means to use each one.

Your initial lesson on self-monitoring will lead nicely into future minilessons for figuring out the tricky words and harder parts. In your next minilesson, you might focus on the idea that as readers dig into more challenging books, they need to be sure they are thinking about the whole story and all the information in their books—not just the words.

> **"Today I want to teach you that readers think about the whole book—the cover, the pictures, and what the book is mostly about—to help them read more challenging books. Readers can think, 'What would make sense?' to figure out the tricky words."**

You could demonstrate this by using a leveled book placed on a document camera or an unfamiliar big book. To start your demonstration, you might point to the book and invite your students to get ready for a challenge. "Readers, today I have a challenging book that we are going to have to work hard to read well together. This book is like the books you are reading during reading workshop time—it is harder and longer (and more interesting) than many of the books we have read before—but I know you are brave enough to dig in with me to give it a try!" Guide students in looking at the front and back covers, reading the title together, thinking aloud about the kind of book it is, what the book will be mostly about, and/or what it might teach. After children turn and talk, you might choose to share some of the ideas about what the book is going to be about: "So as we read the pages in this book and as we come to tricky words we have to think about what this book, as a whole, is about and what would make sense. I heard many of you say that this book is going to be about the many things that students should do and should not do in school, so we can expect to read about these types of things."

As you read on in the book, be sure to demonstrate using the pictures to anticipate what the words might say, and also think aloud about how each new page fits with the title and the book overall. As you read the words, stop and think, saying, "Does this fit with the picture? It does! Does this fit with what is happening in the story? It does!"

To demonstrate solving a hard word, you might mask all or part of a word in the text, forcing you to have to use other sources of information to solve the word. "Whoa! This is really a tricky word!" you might say. "I am going to *have* to use something other than the print. Hmm, . . . Let me check the picture . . . let me think about the title . . . let me think about what's happening in the story . . ." Show kids how they can solve the words in their books using multiple sources of information.

Then give the students an opportunity to try this out in another section of the book where meaning is going to be a key to figuring out a covered word. Reading over the pages, you'll prompt students in the same way you demonstrated prompting yourself. "Oh, here is a tricky word. Think about what the book is about. Check the cover and think, what is this about? Check the pictures and think, what could this word be? What would make sense?" Then you might insert some of the students' options into the sentence, reading it together and asking, "Does this make sense? Does this sound right?" Say something like, "If the word is ___, what do we expect to see at the beginning of the word?" or for more advanced readers, "What do we expect to see at the beginning, middle, or end of the word?"

As you send the students off, you'll want to reiterate the work of this lesson, but also drum up their eagerness to keep working hard through their increasingly difficult books!

Teach kids to continue to use meaning, plus syntax, to problem solve.

If you feel that your readers need more practice holding onto what the text is mostly about, you might decide to teach them to activate their prior knowledge about a topic before they begin reading. As they look at a book's cover, they can think or say, "This reminds me of . . ." or "This is just like . . ." or "I've seen this before . . ." Then, as students read their books, they can use the thoughts they've had about the title, cover, and what they already know about the topic to help them read each page. This strategy is especially useful when kids encounter tricky words. Tell them, "When you get to a word you don't know, you can look at the picture on the page, but if that doesn't help, you can also think about the title and what you know about the topic of the book to help figure it out."

You might even model for readers that they can confirm some of their initial thinking about a topic or book as they move from page to page. For instance, if the book a student is reading is titled *The Playground*, she might read the title and say, "This reminds me of my playground! There's a swing, and a slide, and monkey bars!" Then as she reads each page, she could use that information to confirm what she reads. She might say, "This page has swings on it! I knew there would be a page with swings because I have swings on my playground! This word must be *swing*!"

Many times we prompt children as they are reading to think about "what makes sense, what sounds right, and what looks right," but then find that children don't act on those prompts. Often this is because they don't understand what we mean. Therefore, we have to make sure we are using that language as we teach them how to use these various sources of information. In order to convey how to use meaning to problem solve words, you need to be explicit about what it means when readers ask themselves, "What makes sense?" Teach them, for example, that readers use the illustrations, their prior knowledge, what the book is mostly about, and what they have read so far to answer this question. All of these strategies will lead children to use the meaning of the text as a source of information. By making sure that children are keeping the meaning of the text at the front of their minds, we help them to read with greater accuracy and in turn greater confidence.

You will also want to teach children how to use structure as they are reading to answer the question, "What sounds right for this book?" In other words, you want them to use their oral language, the pattern in the text, or the grammatical structure of the sentence, to predict what words will come next as they read. You can extend the work of attending to syntactical structure during focused shared readings, by turning the students' attention, for example, to verbs and verb tenses. You could cover up a verb like *tell* and give the students two options: *Could this word be* told *or* tell? *Which sounds like a book would sound?* Reread the sentence with each option, allowing the students to hear both choices and to evaluate which one sounds "right." By switching verb tenses students are given word options that hold accurate meaning and similar visual components, which allows students to practice the challenging work of attending to syntactical structures of sentences. It is important to provide the space to notice these syntactical patterns in shared reading so that your readers have a lot of exposure to how books usually sound or go. This will help them to apply the structure or syntax cues in their own books while reading independently. Similar work can be done in shared reading with pronouns, giving students a chance to practice attending to both structure and meaning. *What would make sense here? What would sound right? Could it be the word* her *or the word* she?

Over time, as you teach one strategy, then another for using the prompt, "What sounds right?" you may want to add to an anchor chart each time you return to the concept:

ANCHOR CHART

How do I figure out what sounds right?

- Use the way I talk to think of a word that sounds right.
- Find a word that makes the sentence complete.
- Use the pattern in the book.

Many of the books your students will be reading have very supportive sentence structures that you can teach students to take full advantage of as they read. Explicitly point this out to students in a minilesson, as well as teach them how to use this patterned structure as they problem solve.

> **"Today I want to teach you that once you know the pattern in your book, you can hang on to it as you continue to read the pages. If you forget the pattern, you can always reread from the beginning to get a running start, and use the pictures to help you figure out how the book goes."**

Demonstrate this by showing students how the first few pages of a book may contain a pattern, and once you figure out the pattern (using the pictures, as well as the first few letters of each word, and any known sight words), you can "hang on" to it as you continue to read the pages. As you demonstrate this, you might pretend to forget the pattern, and show students how rereading from the beginning can remind the reader of how the pattern goes.

In another minilesson, you might also demonstrate how to know when the pattern changes, and what to do to figure out the new pages. As you read a predictable, patterned text, stop on each page to self-monitor (as always). Ask yourself, "Did my reading make sense? Sound right? Look right?" On the page where the pattern changes, you might intentionally "mess up" by continuing the pattern from the previous pages. When you pause to self-monitor, you'll say, "Yup, it makes sense. Yup, sounds right to me—I kept the pattern going. But hang on . . . these words don't *look* right. I said 'Look at . . .' but the word here starts with letter *t*. Something's not right. The pattern must have changed! I better try something to fix it."

Differentiate your instruction through conferring and small-group work.

As children read privately and in partnerships, you'll continue to conduct individual conferences and small groups to help them integrate sources of information as they read and address the diverse needs of your readers. In this unit you will want to plan for small groups to help move readers up levels. This is a unit where you can expect your students to move at least one level, if not more. You will, of course, find yourself pulling together groups of children reading at the same level who need extra support to negotiate the level. Remember that as your students become more confident readers, your supports will become lighter and less frequent, as students develop what Marie Clay calls a "self-extending system." This self-extending system includes the internalization of your prompts, so that a child has ways to problem solve on the go. By internalizing your prompts, students learn to detect errors on their own, to try a variety of strategies to correct an error, and then confirm that the new attempt is accurate.

You will also want to pull students who read across levels, yet share a common need. For example, children reading at levels C, D, and E, who are focused on figuring out the words in their books may forget to think about what would make sense and to then look at the letters and parts of words to confirm their guesses. In this case, too, the aim of your teaching will be to help children learn a process of problem solving and then transfer the use of that process throughout their reading work.

Small-group shared reading can also be great support in helping kids integrate sources of information. During small-group shared reading, students can practice monitoring for sense as they read books that are a real challenge. Your goal here will be for students to notice when their reading isn't quite right—closer to the point of error. Reading together with a group makes it clear when your reading doesn't quite work. For example, if there is a picture of a girl drinking from a water bottle and the sentence reads, "Dad put a drink in my bag" but one child reads "Dad put a doll in my bag," the child who miscued will be prompted to notice the mistake right away. Then the children can talk about why the word *drink* looks right, sounds right, and makes sense. Practicing cross-checking requires that the text is a challenge, so shared reading can provide the support readers need, while ensuring they read accurately at these higher levels. By looking across your running records and your conferring notes, you will come to find groups of students who are solely relying on one or two sources of information. Here, too, shared-reading small groups are the chance to pull these kids together to work at using and attending to the neglected source of information.

BEND II: READERS ARE FLEXIBLE PROBLEM SOLVERS

At the start of the unit, you and your students discussed real-life problem solvers. You may have named people or characters in books who were great problem solvers, and you perhaps created a list of qualities that make someone a resourceful problem solver. At the start of this new bend, you might revisit that list of traits and even add to it. Perhaps your original list included "perseverance, never giving up, working together, being fearless, taking risks, and trying new things." Upon returning to this list, you might congratulate your students on working on all these things as readers, and then teach them another trait of a great problem solver—flexibility.

> "Today I want to teach you that readers are great problem solvers. They are resourceful and creative and brave—and they are also incredibly *flexible*. When resourceful readers encounter a problem to solve, they don't just try one thing. They try another, and another, and another. They are flexible problem solvers."

During this portion of the unit, your intentions are twofold. You'll introduce and teach the strategies children need to read proficiently as they move to a higher-level text, and you'll continue to teach children to use these strategies with some flexibility. In other words, you'll do your best to help children avoid the "one-trick pony" syndrome. Often a reader will have lots of success using a particular strategy, say, checking the picture, and so will use it again and again—even if it fails to lead him to read the text accurately, at which point the child is at a loss for what to do. In this bend, then, you'll teach children to draw on all the strategies and skills they've learned this year so that they can fix any problem or challenge they encounter in their texts.

You will teach kids that one try isn't enough. You may explain that when people problem solve, oftentimes it takes many tries until they get it right or solved! Rally your students for this challenge. You might say to them, "Today I want to teach you that readers try out *many* different strategies to help them figure out a tricky word, then they double-check by asking three questions: 'Does it makes sense? Does it sound like a book? Does it look right?' This will help you get the word right. Over the next few days we are going to work really hard to try out many different strategies when we get to a tricky word. We won't just stop after checking the picture. We won't just stop after thinking about what sounds right. And we won't just stop after looking at the letters and thinking about what looks right. We will use *all* that we know to help us solve the tricky words!"

For a lesson like this, you could model from a text whose pictures don't completely give away the tricky word, so that you can show the students what it's like to try a few different strategies and then check your guesses. "Watch as I try this in *The Pond* by Janice Boland (Books for Young Learners). I'm going to check all the charts in our room to remind myself of all the strategies I know before I start to read, so that I can use a few different ones to help me if I need to." You'll have already taught a multitude of strategies in the previous units and in the last bend, and these strategies will be listed on anchor charts around the room.

When you demonstrate all the steps, be sure to narrate for the class what it is that you are doing. You might say something like, "Readers, notice that I got to a tricky word and checked the picture, saying everything I saw, like I always do. The picture didn't help by itself, so I looked at the word's beginning letters. Then I guessed a word that would make sense, but when I reread the sentence, I realized that it didn't sound like a book sounds. Finally, instead of giving up or getting frustrated, I tried again, thought about the whole book, and figured it out. Did you see how I tried lots of different reading strategies and lots of different words, checking each word to see if it made sense, if it sounded like a book, and if it looked right, until I landed on something that worked? That's what I hope *you* always do as readers!"

You may also want to explicitly teach children to use the charts around the room to set goals for themselves and make plans for what they will do to work on the tricky words and hard parts of their books.

> **"Readers, you now know many strategies to try to help you read and understand your books. Today I want to teach you that readers often make plans for the strategies they will try. You can warm up for reading time by rereading all the anchor charts in our classroom. Then you can name the strategies you might use if you get stuck on a tricky part in your book."**

Demonstrate how to "warm up" for reading time by rereading the anchor charts for this unit, as well as old charts that are related to this unit. Then show students how you name a few things you will probably do if you get stuck on a word or if a part of your book isn't making sense, and invite them to do the same. You might even create small copies of charts for students to have at their tables, or keep inside a folder of resources. Some teachers create an "office" for children for doing their reading work by laminating the anchor charts onto a file folder that folds up and stays in the table basket along with the book baggies.

Of course none of this is completely new to your students, nor is it the absolute first time that you have taught a lesson around using multiple strategies, but because this is challenging work for students to take up independently, you will surely want to continue this work across several minilessons and during whole-group and small-group shared reading.

Teach students to use a repertoire of strategies while reading.

During this bend, you'll demonstrate in your minilessons, over and over again, how readers use a whole combination of strategies to tackle tricky words. During follow-up lessons you'll draw on previous anchor charts to incorporate the continual use of multiple strategies to figure out tricky words. You might decide to have children coach you by referring to the chart. They can call out tips or check off whatever strategies they notice you using on smaller individual copies of the chart, and then can turn and tell a partner what else you might try.

By teaching children a variety of strategies and processes for determining which words are tricky, solving those words, and then checking their reading, you will be helping students do high-level thinking work and problem solving. When we hover over our students, waiting for them to make mistakes, pointing out those mistakes immediately and then jumping in to help—and when we ask them to simply apply a given strategy when prompted—we keep our students at a fairly low level of thinking. Instead, you want your children to develop that "self-extending system" that allows them to recognize their own challenges, choose from and try a variety of strategies, and then check their reading independently. This constitutes much higher-level thinking and independence. How important it is, then, that you move mountains to be sure that your children have the mind-set and the tools to tackle tricky words with vigor and independence.

Although you will have taught these strategies several times now, ultimately some of your readers will need additional reminders. When teaching a child who reads levels A/B, whether in a conference or a small group, ask her, "How did you know that word was _____?" The child might say, "Because I see it in the picture." You'll then respond, "How else do you know that it's _____?," prompting her to then use another strategy.

If children have mastered scanning the picture and using the first part of the word, coach them to also check the end of the word. For students to have success in books beyond level D, they will need to start looking across the entire word. Coach them not only to think about what is happening in the text but to say the first part of the word and think about what would make sense. Children who look across a word and only say each individual letter's sound need to "put the sounds together" and again, think about what would make sense and sound right. Your workshop will be loaded with quick small groups each and every day that will help children practice putting these strategies into action.

Teach reading partners ways to help each other solve tricky parts of their books.

During this part of the unit, design your minilessons so that they show how partners can help each other tackle tricky parts. You might start by teaching children that sometimes it's necessary to give a tricky part your best try—*and move on.*

> "Readers, you know, sometimes, no matter what I try, I just can't figure out a tricky word or a tricky part of the text. Today I want to teach you that when that happens, I give it my very best try, and *move on.* I like to use a Post-it to mark those really tricky places so that I can share them with my partner, so we can figure it out together."

You can then teach partners strategies for helping each other through the tricky parts, without simply doing all the work for each other. You will probably want to remind children that they can use all the anchor charts to help them help their partners—especially a chart that lists prompts for MSV. (Does it make sense? Does it sound right? Does it look right?) When children say those three prompts to a partner, they not only help their partner—they are helping themselves internalize the use of all three sources of information any time they need to solve an unfamiliar word.

Partners can also use questions and conversation to help each other through the trickier parts of their books. When children can articulate what is tricky, giving it a name and discussing what is hard, they can learn to recognize that problem each time it arises and eventually come to a solution more quickly. You may want to start a chart of helpful questions partners can use.

Of course, remind your students that readers can ask themselves those questions too!

Use shared reading to support the work of the unit.

Your shared reading plays an integral part in bridging word study with your reading workshop. You'll continue to support students using various sources of information to make sense while reading texts at their level and slightly higher. You may also begin to work on the skills they will need to move up to the next level. The goal is to help children use all sources of information in shared texts so that they transfer the work to their own texts when they encounter difficulty. During shared reading you can check on this and support your kids by saying to them, "Does that make sense? How do you know?" Ask these questions both when their reading makes sense as well as when it does not. This way, children will learn to monitor themselves for coherence. Using clear prompts during shared reading, like the ones you use in guided reading, will help children problem solve independently.

You will also model how to use print strategies to problem solve hard parts and tricky words in texts. Reinforce the strategies that kids are using and will need to move up to higher levels. You may begin to focus on using short vowels, consonant blends, and digraphs. You might have kids "guess the covered word." Help them be resourceful as they do this, cross-checking their guesses for meaning, syntax, and spelling. That is, a child guessing the final word in the sentence "Look at the _____" by looking at a picture of a group of feathered birds might guess *chicken*, based on meaning. But the word is, in fact, *hens*. The child will have to look at the letters in the word to cross-check her original guess. She'll also need to realize that *chicken* or *hen* couldn't be right for referring to more than one bird, so syntactically she'd need to correct it to *hens*, for the group of birds. Similarly, if a child is looking at the sentence, "Look at the hens," the child may recognize the letter *h* and guess *hat*, and will need to guess again using meaning and syntax. In each scenario, encourage kids to give many guesses, rather than a single perfect one.

Differentiate your instruction through conferring and small-group work.

Your higher-level readers may encounter word features (word endings, compound words, or CVC words) or high-frequency words (*come, where, through*) that you have not yet studied as a class. Guided reading is a perfect place to introduce these new features and words. You can give readers cards with their new high-frequency words (or features), and encourage them to practice reading these. Then you might have them look for these in their guided reading text and again in any new texts they read. After your book introduction to the guided reading text, you will spend time coaching each child as he or she reads the text.

Make sure to give lean, consistent prompts that match the level of support the reader needs. After you have heard each child read, reconvene the group. As children talk about the book, assess their comprehension and decide what to teach in order for this group to become independent readers of this new level of text. Students should keep their guided reading books in their baggies and continue to practice them all

week. When you listen to your students read and reread these texts, remember that your level of prompting will become lighter, thus encouraging the development of the self-extending system.

As the rest of your class is moving forward, inevitably some students will still be reading levels A and B. It may be that these children are not yet using initial sounds in words and tend to overrely on pictures. In addition, they may not have built a sight vocabulary large enough to enable them to move to the next level. These children will need your attention. Plan to give them a lot of guided reading instruction in level C books. Their baggies, then, should be transitional ones, full of A/B books they can read independently, as well as C books that you have introduced through guided reading. You may find it helpful to build up your A/B readers' vocabulary by creating mini-text sets to support these children's particular needs.

Students who need help with high-frequency words might read several books with the same repetitive words and patterns, and those who need help with vocabulary in general might read several books about a particular topic so that they encounter the same words again and again, thus committing those to memory. Reading several books with the same words also helps children learn how to use these words in context.

A guided reading session aimed at helping children move up a level typically starts with getting children to think about the meaning of a book. Draw their attention to the cover and the first few pages of the book to consider what it's going to be about. Then, introduce unfamiliar key vocabulary words and have students practice saying and locating the words in the text.

Next, you might focus on the structure of the text (especially if the book language is different than the way children talk). Support students with structure by using the exact language of the text and by rephrasing their ideas into the language of the text. For example, if a child says, "The bear is running," and the text says, "Little Bear ran through the woods," say back to the child, "Yes, Little Bear ran through the woods." Finally, move to the visual information that will be tricky for these readers. This might include pointing out that the print is now two lines instead of one or that print appears above the picture on one page and below the picture on the next. You might introduce new or different punctuation marks that appear in the text as well.

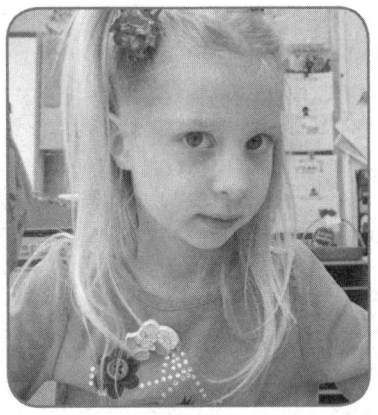

BEND III: READERS MAKE THEIR READING SOUND GREAT!

Launch the bend with a repertoire minilesson, demonstrating how to reread a single text for many purposes.

To launch this bend, you might share examples of people in "real life" who read and reread for many purposes, as a way to drive home the fact that everyone rereads.

> **"Today I want to teach you that *everyone* rereads. Actors and actresses, singers, rock stars, teachers, and *you!* Expert readers are always rereading, for many reasons and many purposes."**

Explain to students that actors and actresses must reread their scripts many times, trying out many different voices and tones to get their reading just the way it needs to be. Or you might talk about singers and rock stars, who practice and practice, rereading and rehearsing until everything is absolutely perfect and ready for performance. You might even talk about yourself! Perhaps you've reread a book many times to get ready for read-aloud or to study for an important exam. Perhaps you have a favorite book that you've reread many, many times, just for the sheer enjoyment of it. Sharing stories of real-life rereading can inspire kids to dive into this part of the unit with enthusiasm.

Of course, there are important reasons for young readers to reread that are very different than the reasons that adults might reread, and these are good for you to keep in mind as you proceed. Each time your beginning readers reread a book, they are gaining practice with recognizing the high-frequency words and spelling patterns that appear in that text. With each rereading they become more and more automatic in their recognition of those words and spelling patterns—this is important work for readers at this level. The high-frequency words and spelling patterns that they learn to recognize with automaticity (in context) will serve them well as they encounter more challenging texts.

In this bend, your main goal will be to teach students how to reread with a variety of purposes. You will help students to increase their intentionality through teaching them to plan, independently and in partnerships, about how they will reread. Students will learn to reread in a multitude of ways: rereading for fluency and expression, fixing tricky words and confusing parts, finding information and important parts, studying and learning about characters, and so on.

Start the bend by setting students up to do a few different things in the first lesson. Rather than an isolated strategy, introduce a repertoire of several strategies at once. Then during independent reading time you can look closely at what students are able to do and which pieces of the repertoire they're focusing on. It's useful to expose students to multiple ways to reread first to assess what they are able to do with ease, and what strategies they need more explicit instruction to understand. This way you are not teaching lessons to students that they do not need, but targeting your instruction for whole-class needs and small groups. In a minilesson, you might say, "Today I want to teach you that readers don't just finish a book and move on to another one. You read your books a few times over trying out different things. You can read through your book the first time trying to get the tricky words right, you can reread a second time trying to make your voice sound smooth, and you can reread a third time looking for places that are fun and interesting that you want to share with your reading partner." You could list these reasons on a chart as a way to ground students in the work.

For a repertoire minilesson, you might demonstrate with an engaging leveled book that lends itself to rereading (because it is short and entertaining), like *Piggy and Dad Play*, from the Brand New Readers series. You will want to demonstrate how you reread this book several times, with a different purpose for each reread. On the first read, you might focus on trying to tackle tricky words. "Watch as I read this book the first time really focusing on all of the words, trying to solve each tricky word using every strategy I can." Then as you quickly make your way through the short book, you'll get students watching for how you reread the book again, but this time with a different focus. "Now notice that I've finished reading the book, but I'm

not going to quickly move onto another. Instead I'm going to reread this same book, but this time I'm going to read it trying to make my voice smooth." Again, you'll demonstrate rereading with this purpose. After you've completed this second reading, you will set them up to watch you reread, yet again, but this time with another purpose—the purpose of finding places that you want to talk to your reading partner about.

After you've demonstrated the process of rereading a book a few times, you'll restate exactly what strategies you used and set the students up to try them as well. In the active engagement part of this minilesson, you might ask children to try these multiple rereads on one of the other stories from the same *Piggy and Dad* series, like *Lemonade for Sale, Play Ball!* or *Water Balloons*.

Teach children that partners can make plans together to reread for many purposes.

As the bend continues, you can shift the focus to ways that reading partners might reread together. Perhaps until now, your reading workshop has always begun with a minilesson, followed by private reading time (reading alone), followed by some time working with a partner. You might alter the routine slightly, giving children time to meet with their partners *before* they read on their own, looking through their books, and making plans for how they will reread their books.

> "Today I want to remind you that careful readers reread with a plan. You and your partner can use special bookmarks as a tool to plan your reading work. You can even invent your own bookmarks to remind you and your partner all the reasons why you would reread."

You might introduce special ready-made bookmarks for partners to use as tools for planning their reading work—each bookmark serving as a reminder for a different familiar way to reread. Partners could make a plan for their reading work, choosing from options listed on their bookmarks:

- Reread this book with a smooth voice.
- Reread to figure out confusing parts.
- Read this book once to figure out the tricky words, then reread again right away.
- Reread to find new information or details.
- Reread to make your voice match the character's feelings.

Of course, any one of these special bookmarks could serve as a stand-alone minilesson to reinforce a particular strategy, introduced on its own, rather than as part of a repertoire. If you haven't previously taught a few of these strategies, then you may want to introduce those one at a time, rather than as a list of familiar choices.

Partners Make Plans

~Reread this book with a smooth voice.

~Reread to figure out confusing parts.

~Read this book once to figure out the tricky words, then reread again right away.

~Reread to find new information or details.

~Reread to make your voice match the character's feelings.

After introducing special bookmarks, and teaching your students how to make plans for their reading with a partner, you might remind children that another way to make plans is to refer to the charts hung around the room to remind them of all the choices they have. It is important that partner time is for reading and talking together, asking and answering questions, and seeking help.

After teaching children a few strategies for making plans together, you might teach a few different ways partners can read aloud the pages together. Working in pairs, children might decide to reread by putting their two voices together to make one smooth voice (reading in unison, but for the purpose of reading smoothly). They may see-saw read, one partner reading a page and the other reading the next page. Or, they might echo read, one partner reading a page, and the other rereading the very same page even more smoothly. Partners might even try reading their books like you read aloud to the class, during which they read a page, then turn the page around and show the pictures to their partner. Don't hesitate to invent ways, or to let students invent ways, for readers to reread their books.

All of these make rereading more engaging and purposeful for children, while also encouraging children to read with increasing automaticity and fluency.

> **"Readers, today I want to teach you that readers read together in many different ways to make their reading sound great. You can read in one voice together, see-saw read, echo read, take turns reading aloud, and even invent new ways to read together."**

Differentiate your instruction through conferring and small-group work.

To reach as many students as possible, you'll identify classroom trends and pull small groups. The above conferences can just as easily turn into small groups to practice the strategies that kids need. You'll probably notice that a select few of your students are still not rereading with a purpose; they are simply reading books and moving on. You might decide to pull these students and give them guided practice with visual reminders about how to reread. The students can then practice reading and rereading the same book a few different ways, before moving onto a second book. This way they get ample opportunity to focus on one text, but trying out the different rereading strategies.

CELEBRATION

To celebrate the work of this unit, you might invite another class to come visit for a reading celebration. Perhaps each one of your students will read aloud to an older partner. Perhaps each one of your partnerships will take turns reading to a visitor or two. Or perhaps you'll highlight what flexible, resourceful problem solvers your students have grown to become by having children draw pictures of themselves solving difficult words, with a few sentences reflecting on what they now do when reading gets tricky. You might display these reflections on a bulletin board, with a pack of Post-its and markers available for visitors to add their own pictures and thoughts on how to handle tricky parts in books. A celebration need not be elaborate for it to be meaningful for your students. Aim to create an experience that allows students to celebrate the strategies they have been practicing: being resourceful readers who have many strategies for word solving.

POSSIBLE TEACHING POINTS

BEND I: READERS THINK ABOUT THE STORY AND ABOUT HOW BOOKS SOUND TO FIGURE OUT WORDS

- "Today we are going to investigate the question, 'How do readers know when they need to go back and fix things up? What are the signs to be on the lookout for?'"

- "Today I want to teach you that readers think about the whole book—the cover, the pictures, and what the book is mostly about—to help them read more challenging books. Readers can think, 'What would make sense?' to figure out the tricky words."

- "Today I want to teach you that readers get themselves ready to read by thinking about what they already know about a topic. As they look at a book's cover, they can think or say, 'This reminds me of . . .' or 'This is just like . . .' or 'I've seen this before . . .' Then on each page of the book, readers use what they already know to help them figure out tricky words."

- "Today I want to teach you that as they read, readers are always asking themselves 'What makes sense?' They use the illustrations, what they already know about the topic, what the book is mostly about, and what they have read so far to answer this question."

- "As they are reading, readers are always asking themselves the question, 'What sounds right?' Readers figure out what word would sound right in that book by thinking about the way it sounds when they talk, the patterns in the book, or how to make the sentence sound like a complete book sentence sounds."

- "Today I want to teach you that once you know the pattern, you can hang on to it as you continue to read the pages. If you forget the pattern, you can always reread from the beginning to get a running start, and use the pictures to help you figure out how the book goes."

- "Today I want to teach you that readers often stop on each page to make sure their reading is making sense. On every page, they ask themselves 'Did my reading make sense? Sound right? Look right?' If you realize that something isn't right, and the pattern changed, it's important to fix it!"

Use this list as a menu of possibilities, selecting only the teaching points that meet the needs of your students. Use your assessment data (running records, conferring and small-group notes, observations, responses to read-alouds, and other information) to decide on a plan that is tailored to the needs of your class. These teaching points may be used as whole-class mini-lessons, mid-workshop teaching points, or for conferences and small-group work. You need not use every teaching point. See the unit overview for guidelines on how much time to spend in each bend.

BEND II: READERS ARE FLEXIBLE PROBLEM SOLVERS

- "Today I want to teach you that readers are great problem solvers. They are resourceful, and creative, and brave—and they are also incredibly *flexible*. When resourceful readers encounter a problem to solve, they don't just try one thing, they try another, and another, and another. They are flexible problem solvers."

- "Today I want to teach you that readers try out *many* different strategies to help them figure out a tricky word, then they double-check by asking three questions: 'Does it makes sense? Does it sound like a book? Does it look right?' This will help you get the word right. It's important though, that readers try out lots of strategies and use all they know to help them solve the tricky words."

- "Readers, you now know many strategies to try to help you read and understand your books. Today I want to teach you that readers often make plans for the strategies they will try. You can warm up for reading time by rereading all the anchor charts in our classroom. Then you can name the strategies you might use if you get stuck on a tricky part in your book."

- "Readers, you know, sometimes, no matter what I try, I just can't figure out a tricky word or a tricky part of the text. Today I want to teach you that when that happens, I give it my very best try, and *move on*. I like to use a Post-it to mark those really tricky places so that I can share them with my partner, so we can figure it out together."

- "Today I want to teach you that reading partners can help each other through the tricky parts, without doing all the work for each other. They can use all the anchor charts, ask each other questions, talk about the tricky parts, and suggest strategies."

BEND III: READERS MAKE THEIR READING SOUND GREAT!

- "Today I want to teach you that *everyone* rereads. Actors and actresses, singers, rock stars, teachers, and *you!* Expert readers are always rereading, for many reasons and many purposes."

- "Today I want to teach you that readers don't just finish a book and move on to another one. You read your books a few times over, trying out different things. You can read through your book the first time trying to get the tricky words right, you can reread a second time trying to make your voice sound smooth, and you can reread a third time looking for places that are fun and interesting that you want to share with your reading partner."

- "Today I want to remind you that careful readers reread with a plan. You and your partner can use special bookmarks as a tool to plan your reading work. You can even invent your own bookmarks to remind you and your partner of all the reasons why you would reread."

- "Today I want to teach you another way that readers make plans for their reading with a partner. They can look at the charts that are hung around the room to remind them of all the choices they have. It is important to remember that partner time is for reading and talking together, asking and answering questions, and seeking help."

- "Readers, today I want to teach you that readers read together in many different ways to make their reading sound great. You can read in one voice together, see-saw read, echo read, take turns reading aloud, and even invent new ways to read together."

Readers Get to Know Characters by Performing Their Books

RATIONALE/INTRODUCTION

Young children are keen observers and actors. They slather suds on their faces in the bathtub so they can pretend-shave, have pretend conversations on pretend telephones, and clip-clop around in too-big shoes. They mimic an authoritative tone while playing house and assume a teacher's voice while instructing a circle of stuffed animals. It is through this kind of role-playing that children come to understand the nuances of differ-ent personae. This character unit capitalizes on children's natural inclination for imitation and role-playing by inviting them to do this same sort of pretending with the characters in their books. As children take on the roles of Piggie and Gerald, Mrs. Wishy Washy and her animals, Ethan and his dad, Biscuit and his friend, and so many others, they will come to know these characters and the stories in which they live, with real intimacy. This unit celebrates that the most important reason to read is for meaning—to bring books to life!

This is a unit perfect for supporting comprehension work with students in beginning reading levels (levels D–G). You might decide to include this unit in your yearlong curricu-lum plans for a number of reasons. For example, for kindergartners, this unit would serve as a perfect extension of the character work introduced in *Becoming Avid Readers* (Unit 4).

Another option for kindergartners is to use Bend III of this unit as an extension to vari-ous "giving the gift of reading" lessons that briefly appear in other units (Units 2, 3, and 4). Giving the gift of reading involves teaching children to rehearse and prepare a read-aloud as a gift for others. If you would like to include extra work on fluent and expressive reading in one of your existing units, you might refer to Bend III.

For first-graders, you may decide that you would like to teach a character unit early on in the year, while kids are reading mostly levels D–G, and then return to character study in *Meeting Characters and Learning Lessons: A Study of Story Elements* (Unit 4) later in the year when kids have moved several reading levels. Or you may decide to supplement Unit 4 using some of the bends in this unit, or perhaps use this unit as a guide for small-group work within that unit.

If you find that a group of your second-graders are reading at F/G during *Series Book Clubs* (Unit 4), then you may want to teach all or some of the bends in this unit to supplement that one, or use this unit to guide your small-group work with those readers.

At any grade level, if most of your students read past level G, then you may want to consider another option. This unit is tailored to beginning readers. If you are looking for a character or fiction unit for transitional readers who read H or above, then you may want to choose the alternate unit (also in this book), "Reading and Role-Playing: Fairy Tales, Folktales, Fables, and Fantasy" instead.

Your students will move on from this unit with a finely developed sense of three story elements (character, setting, and story events) and with a richer understanding of how these three elements, when considered alongside each other, can help them understand characters more deeply.

Meanwhile, although the emphasis of this unit is on comprehension work, you will continue to give readers instruction in using all sources of information—meaning, syntax, and visual—to help them solve words and understand their books.

ASSESSMENT

As you head into a unit on character, you'll want to get a sense of what your students' responses to stories look like. You may have assumed that they should easily be able to figure out how characters are feeling at different points in a story, but might be surprised to discover that some of your children are far more literal than you ever thought.

As a pre-assessment, you might use a whole-class read-aloud or shared reading text that is an end-of-the-year benchmark level text. You can mark several places where you will ask students to turn and talk, stop and jot, or stop and draw their thinking about characters. Because this is a unit geared toward beginning readers, they are likely to also be beginning writers, so you will want to design your prompts so that the responses will be very short, or could be represented in a picture. While this will give you only limited information about the totality of a child's thinking, it will give you broad-strokes information that will be valuable for planning the overall strengths and weaknesses of your class.

At a key moment in the story, you might prompt, "What do you think is going to happen? Jot just a few words or make a quick sketch on your Post-it that shows what you're thinking." At another point in the story, you might prompt, "What do you think the character is thinking right now? Jot that on your Post-it." Later you might prompt, "How does the character feel now? How can you tell?" At the end of the book, you might prompt students write, draw, or retell the major events that happened in the story. As kids begin to write, you might watch for students who find writing their retelling difficult, and ask them to retell the story aloud, or sketch pictures to show what happened instead. Perhaps you'll keep a class list on your clipboard as you circulate, noting who retells in a very literal way, and who retells in a way that demonstrates inferential thinking.

Some teachers prefer to gather this information across several read-alouds, selecting a group of five or six students to listen in on and observe closely each time students to turn and talk to their partners. This is especially helpful if your students are not fluent writers—stopping and jotting, and even sketching, could take too long. If students are not especially strong writers, you won't want to rely on written response as your only source of data.

Whether you assess using writing, drawing, or talking (or a combination of the three), you can then sort your students' responses into general groups of students who will need heavy support in making inferences, students who seem to be making inferences at least some of the time, and students who demonstrate higher-level thinking about the text. It's possible that there is also a group of students that has difficulty responding to the text at all.

At the end of the unit, you can do a similar post-assessment, using another text that is similar in difficulty and length. You can use your notes plus student work to track student progress, and set new goals for future units of study and future read-aloud work.

You will want to consider the kids who have not moved on to level D/E books and be sure that the focus of the unit doesn't sway you from tailoring your teaching especially to their needs. For example, if you have readers who still look only at the beginning letters to figure out what a word says, then your conferences and small-group work with this group will focus not on how to discern character traits, but rather on word solving and using meaning, syntax, and print to figure them out. Look closely at your running records to determine exactly what your students need to move as readers, set a few goals for them that will help them to do so, and incorporate these goals into the unit.

A SUMMARY OF THE BENDS IN THE ROAD FOR THIS UNIT

Essential Question: How can I get to know the characters in my books really well?

- **Bend I: Readers Have Ways to Get to Know a Character**

  How can I read and notice lots of things about characters—the things they do, how they feel, and what they think?

- **Bend II: Partners Pretend They Are Characters and Perform Books in Clubs to Become Character Experts**

  How can I reread and act out my books with my partner in ways that help me understand and express things about the characters? How can I reread my books many times with my book club, thinking about the different ways we can be our characters?

- **Bend III: Giving the Gift of Reading**

  How can I read and reread my books to get ready to share them with an audience? How can I make the characters and the stories come to life?

In Bend I (Readers Have Ways to Get to Know a Character), you'll teach students strategies to get to know a character well and to describe what that character does in a story. You'll invite students to think of characters in books as friends for life—they only need to open the pages of a book anytime they want to see that friend. They'll learn to pay attention to how characters feel, as well as other story elements to get to know the characters in their books. You may decide to spend up to two weeks in this bend.

In Bend II (Partners Pretend They Are Characters and Perform Books in Clubs to Become Character Experts), children will spend a few days learning to think and talk more about characters in their partnerships, making inferences and growing ideas about them as they role-play and act out parts of their books, using what they know about each character to infer what they might think and say beyond the pages of the text. Midway through the bend they will shift to an exciting new structure, spending a week in character book clubs, dramatizing what's happening in their stories in order to extend their thinking about characters.

In Bend III (Giving the Gift of Reading), children will give each other and an audience the gift of reading by preparing a text to perform. This bend extends similar work introduced in sessions and celebrations that appear in other units of study. You should be able to wrap up the unit of study in just one week.

GETTING READY

Gather books featuring central characters, at students' reading levels.

To prepare for this unit, search your leveled library for books that feature characters: people, animals, or even anthropomorphized objects. PM Reading by Rigby has some engaging titles for level B–E readers, as does Candlewick Press's series Brand New Readers. Even with the easiest-level books, which have relatively undeveloped and mostly unnamed characters, children can use illustrations, the plot, and any relevant background knowledge to learn about characters. For levels F/G the Biscuit series by Alyssa Capucilli and the Elephant and Piggie series by Mo Willems (and other books like them) are popular character books.

However, you need not have an extensive collection of series books for this unit. You can group books by broader character categories as well: animal characters, friends, families, characters who travel, characters at play, pets, farms, characters at school, and characters who cook are just a few categories you might find in a typical classroom library at levels A–G. If you have multiple copies of any titles, certainly put them together in these baskets so that partners and groups of children can read the same books together, making it much easier to talk about and dramatize parts of the text. These multiple copies within category-based and series-based baskets of books will become especially helpful in the third bend, when children participate in book clubs.

At the start of the unit, you might encourage students to shop for books alongside their reading partner, so that they might select at least a few of the same titles to talk about and dramatize. Not to worry if you haven't got many multiple titles, though. The books your children are reading are short enough that they can easily read the whole book together, and then talk and act parts out during partner time.

In the third bend, you will want to strategically group kids into clubs of four students, preferably by simply matching up two partnerships. For that portion of the unit, you may want children to select books for their book baggies as a group, or perhaps you'll decide to have clubs choose or create a basket of character books from your classroom library to share.

Choose shared reading, read-aloud, and other books to use as demonstration texts throughout the unit.

To launch this unit, we recommend revisiting all your favorite familiar characters from books you've read aloud or used for shared reading in the past. You may want to prepare for this by setting out these favorite books along the top of your bookshelf or on some other display, or by pulling out old charts from those read-alouds, or creating a new chart that lists all the familiar characters your students already know. You'll refer to your old read-alouds often at the start of Bend I.

Once you have gathered your familiar character read-alouds and shared-reading texts, select a shared-reading book that you might thread through the unit. Big books, such as the Mrs. Wishy-Washy series by Joy Cowley or the Brand New Readers lap books published by Candlewick Press work well. Additionally, you'll want to select a read-aloud or leveled book or two to use as a demonstration text in your minilessons, such as *Are You Ready to Play Outside?* from the Elephant and Piggie series by Mo Willems (level F/G). Choose texts at a level so that your minilesson demonstrations will match closely to the work kids will do as they read both independently and with a partner.

Of course, it's also important that you continue to read aloud engaging picture books that have complex characters you can discuss as a class. A couple we love are *Lilly's Purple Plastic Purse* by Kevin Henkes, *The Recess Queen* by Alexis O'Neill, *Mr. Tiger Goes Wild* by Peter Brown, and *When Sophie Gets Angry* by Molly Bang. Have fun finding your favorites!

Strategically match children up—first in partnerships, and then in clubs.

For the first two bends, your reading workshop time will be structured the usual way: a minilesson, private reading time, and then a bit of time each day for kids to read and talk about books with a partner, ending with a share to wrap up the day's work. Then, in the third bend, you'll create groups of four children (by putting two existing partnerships together) who will read together in book clubs. These clubs will most likely be level-based (homogeneous) groups, so that kids can share and swap books easily. A straightforward way to do this is to assign two separate partnerships to a group, forming a club of four. This has the advantage that each partnership will have already had plenty of practice together. However, you might decide that some individuals will benefit from being in a group with new children, or children who read a level or two harder, or a level or two easier. You'll also want to take into account children's speaking and listening skills as much as their reading levels for this part of the unit—it really won't do to group four children who all read the same level—but will not talk to one another about the books!

BEND I: READERS HAVE WAYS TO GET TO KNOW A CHARACTER

Launch the unit with a classroom "This is your life" experience. Take a walk down memory lane revisiting all their favorite characters from past read-alouds.

On the first day of this unit, you might help children recall favorite characters from past read-alouds. You might display the covers of each read-aloud on a clothesline and ask each student to place a Post-it on their favorite book. Or instead, you might decide to create a chart listing favorite characters, with a picture next to each character and a few words describing the character's traits. Alternatively, you might decide to go all out and invite a colleague or guest to come dressed as a favorite character (or two, or three!) to kick off the unit. After jogging kids' memories and getting them jazzed up about favorite characters, you might then invite them to think about characters as friends. "Once you know a character from a book, they are friends for life," you might tell your students, "and all you have to do, for the rest of your life, to see that friend again, is open up an old book and reread." Then open up their most favorite read-aloud of all from the school year so far, and reread, pausing to think aloud and talk about the character: her feelings, her personality traits, how she changes across the story, and if she (or other characters) learn any lessons in the story.

Teach children a few specific strategies they can use to read in ways that yield deeper comprehension.

After launching the unit, you might tell students that in this unit, they'll be meeting many new friends—that is, characters. Let them know that they'll be learning how to really get to know each character, and that it all starts even before they open the pages of the book. Begin by briefly revisiting the book walk, focusing on how to get ready to read a story. You might model with a simple book like *Are You Ready to Play Outside?* (Level F/G) by Mo Willems. Teach your students to use the title, the cover illustration, and the title page to acquaint themselves with the characters.

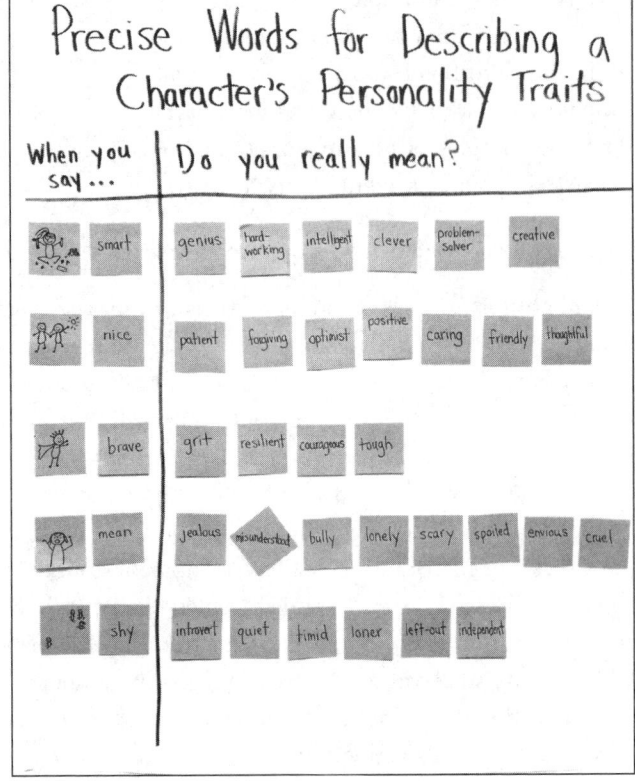

> **"Today I want to teach you that when readers want to get to know the characters in a new book they use the title of the book, the cover illustration, the title page, and even the back of the book to get themselves ready to read. They ask themselves, 'What does this tell me about the character(s)? How might this story go?'"**

Demonstrate by saying, "The title of this book (hold it up for children to see) is *Are You Ready to Play Outside?* Hmm, . . . Right away I see an elephant, and he looks happy. His hands are in the air and he's smiling. And in the background is a little pink pig—she looks happy too. I'm thinking that maybe they are going to play outside because the title says a little something about that."

Then, show children how you preview the title page: "Let me turn to the title page. Ah. Here they are again. This time the elephant is holding a bullhorn and he's shouting the title, written as a speech bubble. He's shouting 'Are you ready to play outside?' to the little pig, who looks like she's on her way. I'm thinking they must be friends."

Last, demonstrate using the back of the book. In this case the blurb on the back of the book nicely sets up the story, and gives readers the characters' names, and clues about their personalities.

> Gerald is careful. Piggie is not. Piggie cannot help smiling. Gerald can. Gerald worries so that Piggie does not have to. Gerald and Piggie are best friends.

As you read the back of this (or any book you decide to demonstrate with), think aloud saying, "Hmm, . . . Now I know a little bit about the characters. Let me think, how might this story go?"

Revisit strategies readers use to engage with the characters and the story.

Another helpful skill to revisit is accumulating text across pages so students are able to say not just what they learned about a character on each page but also what all the pages together can teach about a character. For example, if students were to just focus on the cover picture of *Are You Ready to Play Outside?* then they might say, "Gerald the Elephant and Piggie are happy!" Yet if they accumulated the story across pages—they'd be more likely to say, "Gerald is working hard to make Piggie happy. First he shelters her from the rain. Then he makes it rain!" You can emphasize that readers' ideas about characters sometimes change as they read on and learn more, synthesizing the information they learn across pages.

In these early-level books, it is also important to pay attention to the ending. You might teach children to ask themselves, "How might the character feel now?" or "What might the character be thinking now?"

> "Today I want to teach you that readers often put themselves in the characters' shoes to imagine what they are thinking and what they would say. They can role-play with a partner to make the characters talk and think."

For example, on the last page of *Are You Ready to Play Outside?* the text reads, "Elephants make the best friends." In the picture, Gerald, the elephant, is showering Piggie with water, spouting from his trunk. In a minilesson, you might invite children to pay special attention to this page—both to the picture and the text—to figure out how the characters feel and infer what they may be thinking. Kids will likely realize that this is a story about friendship, and about making the most of things. They might say, "I think Piggie feels happy 'cause she and Gerald found a way to be happy, rain or shine," or "Piggie is happy now even though things didn't go exactly the way she wanted." Then readers may learn to role-play to make the characters talk and think. A child role-playing Gerald might say, "I'm thinking that I'm happy as long as Piggie is happy." Piggie might say, "I love my best friend. He's the best."

During this first bend of the unit, you'll steer children to focus especially on a book's illustrations, paying close attention to characters' facial expressions, body language, and gestures because these can reveal quite a bit about their moods, personalities, and feelings. For example, a child who notices that a character keeps making googly eyes might conclude, "Piggie always makes funny faces. What a silly pig she is!"

In addition to thinking about how pictures and text work together to tell a story, nudge students to think about how pictures and text together reveal something about characters. You might say, "Today, I want to teach you that readers look at the pictures and the words together because they know that the two work hand-in-hand to tell readers something about the characters. Readers can learn what characters are doing, what they are thinking, and what they are feeling."

As children look closely at the pictures and read the words to get to know characters, it will be important to revisit or introduce the print strategies appropriate for the reading levels in your class. For example, you may need to do minilessons or small groups highlighting that when readers come to a tricky word, they can work to figure it out. Readers check the picture to think about what is happening in the story, imagine a word that would make sense, then look at the word all the way to the end to see if it looks right as well. This cross-checking work is very important as children move up in levels. For example, a level E reader needs to cross-check with an emphasis on meaning (Does it make sense?), structure (Does it sound right?), and graphophonic information (Does it look right?). As children move up in levels, they will need to attend to internal parts of words and not read only letter by letter.

Spotlight studying other story elements to learn more about a story.

You'll also want to draw children's attention to other story elements to help them contextualize their understanding of the characters in their books. You may ask, "Where is the character right now? What is she doing there?" to help students visualize both the character and the setting. Push their thinking about how the character and setting are connected by asking, "How does the setting change the way the character might say or do something?"

> **"Readers, today I want to teach you that as you're reading, you can stop and think about how the setting influences the character. You can think, 'Where is the character right now? What is she doing there?' Make a picture in your mind of where she is and what's she's doing. Think: 'How does the setting change the way the character might say or do something?'"**

In *Are You Ready to Play Outside?* it's clear that the story takes place outdoors and the setting (the weather) plays a major role in the story. The main problem in the story, after all, is that it is raining, and Piggie and Gerald want to play outside. When it begins to rain, Piggie becomes very angry, and so the setting has a very clear effect on how the characters feel and talk. An obvious example like this is helpful to use to help children understand that the setting in a story often influences the events, as well as the characters' thoughts, feelings, and actions. Kids often need a reminder to consider the setting, and to keep track of where characters are, and if the setting changes at all. This work doesn't seem like much in levels A–G, but it is wise for children to practice this work now as readers, so that in harder, longer books, they are already accustomed to thinking about *all* the story elements as they read.

Set children up to work meaningfully in partnerships.

In this bend, during partner time, students could work on retelling what their books are about—even after they have just read them. Reconstructing the text is ideal partner work. Some kids might do a retelling before they read the text to their partner and then afterward the two can work together to name the important events. They can use the cover, title, and pictures to say what happened in the story as a way to support their retelling. Another way to help children retell is to teach them to answer the questions, "Who is in the story?" and "What did she do, or what happened to her?" Of course, whenever it is difficult to retell, readers can go back to the last place where everything was still making sense and read from there to pay closer attention to what is happening.

In addition to retelling, you can add to children's partner talk repertoire the option of discussing what they noticed about the characters in their books. Remind children that just as they did on their own, they can work with a partner to look at characters' facial expressions, their gestures, and their actions, to learn about them. They can describe how characters are feeling at the beginning, middle, and end of a book, as well as what they do and don't say in order to get to know them inside and out. You might decide to start an anchor chart to support partner talk about characters. As the unit goes on, you can add to it:

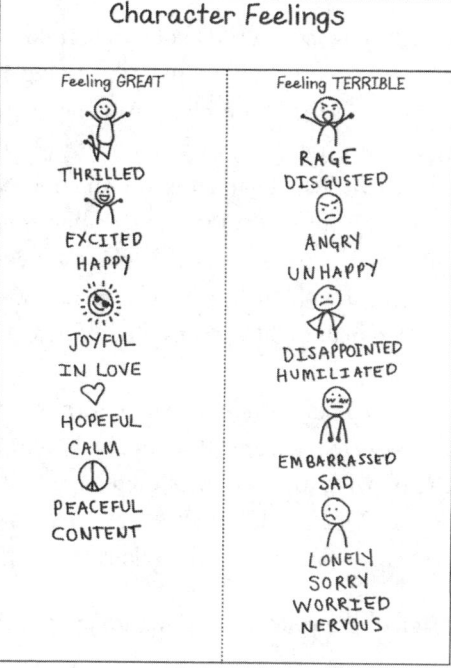

ANCHOR CHART

Partners Talk about Characters

- "The character looks . . ."
- "The character feels . . ."
- "The character said . . . The character didn't say . . ."
- "At the beginning . . . in the middle . . . in the end . . ."

As children work together, keep an eye out for how well they are able to listen and respond in a partnership or a group. Then, you can decide on some next steps to support them with these conversational skills. Keep in mind that children will have a same-level partner and will rely on a repertoire of things they can do together as they read and talk and bring their books to life.

Many teachers find it helpful to create charts that display a variety of vocabulary words for talking about feelings, with picture clues from familiar books, or photographs of children, to help children use precise language when they describe their characters. Instead of saying, "She's sad," they might say, "She's feeling very frustrated right now!" Then, during partner time, encourage students to respond and build on what their partners say.

Invite children to figure out what characters *might* be saying or thinking based on what's happening in the story.

Because so many of the books your children are reading have very little text per page, they will often need to infer what a character might be saying or thinking. Children could write speech or thought bubbles on Post-its that they then place over the characters in their books to show what they think their characters are thinking or saying on each page. Teach students: "Sometimes the book does not come right out and tell you what the characters are thinking. Sometimes you have to figure it out on your own! To show what you think your characters are thinking, you can add speech bubbles or thought bubbles on Post-it notes, right into the pages of your books!" You could use *Are You Ready to Play Outside?* to demonstrate this as, conveniently, the text is largely in the form of speech bubbles—which can be used as examples of what children might add into other books using Post-its, and the pictures provide support for figuring out how the characters feel.

As they read, students will inevitably come across tricky parts or difficult words. Sometimes words are just tough to read, and other times they are words children have never before encountered. When students read on their own and they come across these parts, they can mark them and bring them to a partner to discuss. Meanwhile, you'll want to teach them strategies to deal with tricky words and parts on their own, and remind kids to be on the lookout for these when they work with partners.

Differentiate your instruction through individual conferences and small-group work.

As you support your readers in moving up the trajectory of text levels in your classroom, you will want to make sure that you are not only helping them to reread and think about their books but also still encouraging them to word solve and work through tricky parts. Emphasize that they use what is happening in the story and what they know about the characters to help them think about what a word may mean. Have kids reread tricky sections thinking about all that they know about what the character is doing and what they may want. Then, as they come to the tricky part, have them say the first part of the word and think about what would make sense. Then have them check the ending or read through all parts of the word. It's important to help readers deal with difficulty, using what they know about the story and characters not just to think and talk but to word solve and get through tough parts of their books.

Support the work of this bend through shared reading and read-aloud.

Throughout this bend, you will use your shared reading and read-aloud times to scaffold children's work. You might gather your class around a big book or a read-aloud you've already read several times. Set children up to take on particular roles, such as that of the narrator and the characters in these familiar stories. You can ask, "So right now, while you are sitting here, will each of you be Mrs. Wishy-Washy? You just washed the animals and now they're back out in the mud. What would you say to them if you were Mrs. Wishy-Washy? Say it with feeling!"

You'll find this works really well, especially if you model a time or two, reading with exaggerated facial expressions and gestures. In parts where there is dialogue, have children repeat the lines after you, mimicking your dramatic interpretation. In parts where there are no lines of dialogue, show children how they can imagine lines for their characters based on the inferences they make from illustration details and the story line.

BEND II: PARTNERS PRETEND THEY ARE CHARACTERS AND PERFORM BOOKS IN CLUBS TO BECOME CHARACTER EXPERTS

Teach children to role-play their characters, to support comprehension work.

In the first bend, you taught your students to use clues in the text and illustrations to infer, to learn about the things that characters do and say, and to begin imagining what a character *might be* thinking and feeling. Now, in the second bend of this unit, you'll push this work further by teaching students how to embody characters—to pretend to be them.

At this point, you've likely taught specific ways to get to know characters and also engaged the class in a dramatic read-aloud—where you've provided scaffolded opportunities for children to act like the characters. You might have invited children to play the role of a character in a book, first setting up the scene and then nudging kids to step into the character's shoes, thinking, feeling, and acting as he does. Perhaps you supported children with prompts like, "Say it like he's saying it!" or "Don't *tell* us how he feels—*show* us!"

After a number of these kinds of experiences, you might say to your students, "Oh wow, you all are so good at becoming the character as you read! How about if we spend a few days reading every book as if we're the characters? Only instead of doing this as a whole class, and on your own, you will work with your partner. You'll read your books together as if they are scripts and you are putting on a mini-play. Do you think you could become a character—to think to yourself, 'I bet she's really mad now,' and then give the character's words an angry tone? And could you notice when the character's feelings might be changing, and make sure the voice in your head and your read-aloud voice change to show that?"

> "Today I want to teach you that one way readers get to know the characters in their books really well is to become those characters as they read. Readers walk in the shoes of their characters, noticing when they are feeling a certain way, and then bring those feelings into their voices and gestures as they are reading and acting out the story."

As you begin your minilessons for this bend, you might find it helpful to include a few children in a demonstration of how partners can act out scenes from texts together, with one child as the character and the other as the narrator of the story. Teach children that the narrator's job is to read the text that is not a "talking part." Your students will develop a more sophisticated notion about dialogue, quickly identifying the talking parts through the punctuation.

Show children how it looks when partners read a book together, each pretending to be a character or the narrator and then making the character or narrator come alive with expressive voices and dramatic gestures as they read. In early-level books with characters that don't talk, teach children to infer what the character would say and think. Your teaching point could be: "Today, I want to teach you that when you and your partner are acting out books, and you come to a part where a character doesn't say anything, you can think, 'Hmm, . . . What might the character say in this part?' and then look closely at the pictures to help you imagine those words."

For example, in a list book about a school day, if the text says, "We draw/We write/We play" and so on, children can imagine what the kids on those pages might be saying. To model this, on the "We draw" page, you might say, in an expressive voice, "Ooh, I love to draw. I'm drawing a picture of a unicorn to give to my mommy when I get home. Where's the yellow crayon?"

As children put on these mini-plays, they will relay their understanding of story elements, giving you a chance to assess not only their ability to retell but also their understanding and interpretation of character.

Support the work of this unit through read-aloud.

As you near the end of this bend, you may want to shift your emphasis during read-aloud time toward whole-class conversations in which children learn how to talk back to texts and make connections between the characters of different books. Children can notice what is similar or different about characters in some of the books that you've read aloud as a class.

During read-aloud, your students should be able to act out a page or more in a book while pretending to be the character (or assuming the role of narrator), using their voice, expressions, and gestures in ways that match what they know and think about the character.

Decide how to get organized for book clubs.

During the first part of this bend, you modeled how to pretend to be a character from a book using all the clues from the text. You provided opportunities and guidance so that children could pretend to be characters and narrators in the company of their partners. Now you'll up the ante for the work of getting to know characters well. The work in the remainder of the bend will take place within the structure of book clubs. The goal is that children come to understand their characters in deeper ways.

You have some options as you continue on in this bend. You could create character-specific book clubs—the Puppy Mudge series by Cynthia Rylant, Maisy books by Lucy Cousins, the Mrs. Wishy-Washy series by Joy Cowley, the characters in the Brand New Readers series published by Candlewick Press, Piggie and Elephant by Mo Willems—or you could create baskets around types of characters, such as "Animal Characters," "Friends," "Families," "Characters Who Travel," "Pets," "Farm Characters," "Characters at School," and "Characters Play Together." The latter method will be a better option if texts are limited. Whatever you decide, plan to sort books before this bend begins. In addition, you will need to decide how and when kids will meet with their club members. Will they meet with a partner every day? Will they perform their books as a group twice a week?

Introduce children to the work of becoming a character expert.

Tell your students that the big secret to becoming a character expert is to know the story of the character very well. Explain to students that they will be doing this work in book clubs.

> "Sometimes readers work with other readers, in book clubs. You can work with the readers in your club to get to know the characters in your books so well that you can make them your own. As you read and reread your books together, be sure to look at both the *words* and the *pictures*, and pay *close* attention to what the character does and says."

Emphasize that rereading is an important part of the work they will do, both to perform their books and to understand their characters better. Practicing reading a book for a performance builds fluency.

Over the course of this bend, you'll share the many purposes for rereading, and highlight how rereading can help make stories come alive. You might introduce, one-by-one, a few ways for your students to make their reading more and more expressive and dramatic. In one minilesson you might simply emphasize reading to make the text sound smooth (scooping up the words into phrases instead of word by word). In another minilesson, you might focus on making your voice sound like the characters' voices, and changing your voice to match each character's feelings across the book. In yet another minilesson, you might teach kids how to read like a professional storyteller, with props and gestures and sound effects. And finally, you might teach students how to "pop out" important parts by slowing down and putting emphasis on some sentences more than others, and making use of dramatic pauses. With each new minilesson, you might add to a chart.

You'll send kids off each day to do this work in clubs, comprised of clusters of four kids sharing a basket of books. As you observe your class, you will see kids in each club engaging in reading aloud to one another for many purposes—dramatizing their books in mini-performances that help them understand their books. You'll also probably find that having a mini-audience in their club members makes reading a time that is purposeful and engaging for everyone.

Invite children's varied interpretations and mini-performances of books.

As they engage in mini-performances of their books, readers might try out different ways to sound and act like their characters, and then decide on a way that best matches the clues the text provides. Club members will negotiate their varied interpretations of the character with each other, saying things like, "You said that with a silly voice. Look at her face on this page. She doesn't like it when Ruby kisses her. She's frowning. I think she's mad. So she wouldn't say it in a silly way. She'd say, 'Yuck,' in a mad way. Can you say it more mad-like?" On the surface, children will appear to be simply acting out parts of the story, but in fact, they'll be engaged in important work. While children "play" with text, they will make meaning, use a wide variety of reading strategies, negotiate interpretations, and "publish" their understandings through mini-performances.

As the bend progresses, teach children how to perform different versions of the same book by asking themselves, "What could go differently?" They might think, "The feelings of the characters could be different from what we thought they were in our first performance. Let's act out the book with different feelings."

For example, in the simple book, *I Am*, by Jillian Cutting, the text reads, "I am jumping/I am climbing . . ." and so on. The illustration on each page includes the same character doing the action mentioned in the text. One child might interpret this girl as having fun while playing in her backyard, while another child might say, "She's so lonely. She's all by herself. I think she got in trouble and couldn't have a playdate." These two interpretations will lead kids to act out the story twice, each time with distinct intonations, expressions, and gestures.

You might teach children to extend the "script" for their mini-performances to act out scenes that are beyond what's on the pages. Readers could predict what might happen after the end of the story, and say to themselves, "Given what I know about her already, what could I expect her to do next?"

> **"Today I want to teach you that one thing readers do is act out scenes that are beyond what's on the pages; they act out what might come after the last page of the book. At the end of a story, you can use what you know about the character to make a good prediction about what might happen next, even though the story is over."**

For example, the last page of the book *I Am* includes the words "I am sleeping," with an illustration of the girl on a hammock. You might say, "Readers, imagine when this little girl wakes up. Given what you know about her, what do you think she would say? What might she want to do?" The children who think she's having fun in her backyard might imagine the girl saying, "That was a good nap. Now it's time to play again. What should I do?" The kids who think she must have gotten in trouble and has to play by herself might imagine the girl saying, "This is so boring. I wish I could have a friend over. I can't believe I have to play alone again. I can't wait until tomorrow when my friends can play here!"

It is vital to honor multiple interpretations of a text, while also holding kids accountable for grounding their interpretations in what the text and their own experiences offer. You can model this during read-aloud. Choose a book like *Two of a Kind* by Jacqui Robbins, and suggest that different readers will interpret the characters' intentions, behaviors, and actions in a variety of ways. For example, some readers might think that Kaylie and Melanie are mean girls who tease others and act exclusive, while other readers think that Kaylie and Melanie may simply be jealous of Anna and Julisa. Then model how to pull evidence from the text to support each interpretation.

This modeling will position children to bring the same sort of interpretative thinking to their work in clubs. As children act out their books, they will then bring the understanding that characters—just like real people—are complex. As they try out one interpretation and then another, they will be doing advanced character analysis work and high-level cognitive work.

BEND III: GIVING THE GIFT OF READING

Throughout this unit, your students have learned to look at text and illustrations closely to understand the characters in their books. They have imagined themselves as characters, stepping into their shoes to gain a deeper understanding of what makes their characters tick. Your students have also played around with story elements, thinking about how these changes affect the characters they have come to know so well and acting out their own interpretations of the books in book clubs. In this final bend, your students will work in clubs to revise and shape their mini-performances from the last bend in preparation for a grand finale performance to share with families and friends.

Throughout their lives, your children have received the gift of reading from adults. In this final bend, you'll give them the opportunity to give that gift back. You might say, "Readers, we have come to a very special time of the year. So far, most of your reading lives have come from what other people have given you. You've been given books that you love and taken to the library. You've been pulled onto laps and into chairs to snuggle around stories. Here in school, you've been read to, too, and, of course, you've read along with others. And you've spent the past few weeks bringing your stories to life! Well, guess what? You now have something to give back. For the next few days, you'll work really hard to make your performances as strong as they can be, and then, you'll have the chance to give the beautiful gift of reading back to all of the people who matter most to you—your family. For a little while, we will transform our reading workshop into a gift workshop. So, let's get to work making our gifts!"

> **"Today, I want to teach you that you can give the gift of reading! You can think about the people you care about and which stories they would love to hear from you. You can decide what you will perform, how you will perform it, and who will be your audience."**

Invite children to make decisions about their performances.

Children have been doing the work of practicing and performing for others throughout the unit, and now they must make decisions about their final performance—which text will they perform? Will they perform the exact words from a text or choose to perform an interpretation? It is up to students to decide which version of their text is most compelling. This will be the one they perform for the celebration. As children make these decisions, suggest that they revisit their books closely, seeing it first one way, then another, and then performing it several different ways. Once clubs have practiced and chosen the way their books will go, give them the stage and let them show off their new performing skills for one another!

Help children set reading and performance goals, and set them up to support one another.

Work with students to set goals for growth as readers and performers and to help them put finishing touches on their performances. Children can then meet with their clubs to work on these goals. Some groups may decide that they will work on picturing the characters better and using more gestures as they read. Other groups might focus on volume and stamina, making goals for how many times they will read each book, and how they plan to rehearse each day.

To support club work, teach children a routine for how to support each other's reading goals. Teach them that when clubs get together, they decide who will go first. The club member who goes first can announce the goal she is working on and then try to reach it as she reads a book out loud. When she is done reading, her club members can offer her feedback on how she did. Maybe they will ask questions. They might also give each other little tips, like, "When it comes to stopping and thinking during reading, you did that best in the second book." Then it's time to switch roles. In this way, students will work together to get their reading ready to give to someone else as a gift.

Reinforce children's self-monitoring and fix-up strategies.

Extend the idea that book club members can help each other by suggesting that readers, too, can be their own partners, helping themselves. One way readers do this is by self-monitoring and using fix-up strategies. Once you have reminded children to self-monitor, they also need to self-correct.

> "Today I want to teach you that when you are presenting your gift reading, you will want to make it as beautiful as possible. Sometimes, though, it will not be perfect. You will mess up. But, that's okay because you can use rereading to fix it. Your listener will understand. Messing up happens to everyone. You will just need to say, 'Let me try that again,' then reread that whole sentence or page."

Teach children that if they are stuck on a word, they can back up and get a running start toward that word. The running start can involve remembering what they read so far, or getting the language structure going again to help them jump the tricky word hurdle. Tell your readers that self-corrections are one of the most important signs that they are growing as readers. That's not an exaggeration. Self-correcting, whether it is successful or not, is a sign that children are self-monitoring. So many students do not fix up their reading; they just ignore the errors. Now is a good time to reinforce self-correcting as both a behavior and a reading strategy. Not only will this support students' foundational skills, it will also prepare them to move up into texts of higher complexity.

Prepare children for the final celebration.

The unit ends with a reading celebration. Children will give the gift of reading to someone in their lives. Children will choose an audience from outside the classroom—parents, caregivers, or friends. If their audience isn't able to make it to the classroom performance, tell children that they can bring the gift directly to their loved ones (after all, what you've really set them up to do is to show off their reading and dramatization skills, which they can do anywhere). Don't forget to give these children the opportunity to bring their books home to read to their chosen recipients. You might even draft a note as a class, explaining the gift, so that family members understand the importance of this reading. Children whose loved ones weren't present for the performance could later report how their gift-giving went and how their audience reacted.

Some children might choose to give the gift of reading to several different people, using the same book. Each recipient will undoubtedly leave your student with another way to think about and appreciate that same book. In this way, your students will learn that multiple reads lead to deeper understanding.

As you help children prepare for the grand finale, you will, of course, remind them of all that they have learned. Taking cues from books can be a very detailed process—children can think about each word, considering why the author chose that word and how it should be read. They can reread a specific line on a page, trying out different ways it might sound. They might make a line or a word louder or softer; they might try a line or a word slower or faster. They can think about whether it sounds better to take big breaths or little breaths in between words as they read. Children can pretend to be each other's audience and offer tips as they listen. Meanwhile, you could set them up to do this kind of work in the writing workshop, too. They can reread to practice their written pieces for the upcoming celebration.

> **"Today, I want to teach you that as performers get ready to share the gift of reading through a performance, they have decisions to make: will they use the exact words of the book or make up their own? How will they act out the characters? Performers try out different ways to figure out how to share their book with an audience!"**

You might also teach children to plan for turn-and-talks. They can use Post-its to mark places where they can stop reading and engage in an interaction with their gift recipient. They might point out details in their pictures, make sound effects or facial expressions to communicate meaning, or read certain pages more than once. They could revisit previously read pages, especially when the current page connects with the prior ones in some important way. They could stop to say what they are thinking about at a certain part, and they could ask their listener to share what he or she is thinking, too. This is an effective way to teach the crucial concept that readers think while they are reading, thereby discovering meaning.

CELEBRATION

So long as your children have the opportunity to step back and see the work that they've done in the unit, celebrations need not be elaborate affairs. This celebration, though, should feel different from the others you've had before. Your children's gift-giving will leave an impression on their guests that is sure to last long past the celebration itself.

Remind students to continue reading and giving gifts to their loved ones even after the unit ends. Send them home with bags full of books, poems, charts, interactive writing pieces, copies of their "gifts," keep books (http://www.keepbooks.org/), and shared reading materials that you have read together. Send your children off feeling strong and proud about their achievements so that they read even more on their own.

BEND I: READERS HAVE WAYS TO GET TO KNOW A CHARACTER

- "Readers, one of the best parts about reading is all the new friends you make in your books. Today I want to teach you that once you know a character from a book, that character is a friend for life! All you have to do, for the rest of your life, to see that friend again, is open up an old book and reread."

- "Today, I want to teach you that when readers want to get to know the characters in new books they begin by using the title of the book, the cover illustration, the title page, and even the back of the book to get themselves ready to read. They ask themselves, 'What does this tell me about the character(s)? How might this story go?'"

- "Readers, today I'd like to teach you that readers don't just think about each page separately. They hang on to what they have read across all the pages, and think about what all the pages combined might teach about a character. Sometimes readers' ideas about characters change as they read on and learn more."

- "Today I want to teach you that the ending of the book can also teach you a lot about the characters. Readers ask themselves, 'How might the character feel now?' or 'What might the character be thinking now?'"

- "Today I want to teach you that readers often put themselves in the characters' shoes to imagine what they are thinking, and what they would say. They can role-play with a partner to make the characters talk and think."

- "Today, I want to teach you that readers look at the pictures and the words together because they know that the two work hand-in-hand to tell readers something about the characters. Readers can learn what characters are doing, what they are thinking, and what they are feeling."

- "Readers check the picture to think about what is happening in the story, imagine a word that would make sense, then look at the word all the way to the end to see if it looks right as well."

- "Readers, today I want to teach you that as you're reading, you can stop and think about how the setting influences the character. You can think, 'Where is the character right now? What is she doing there?' Make a picture in your mind of where she is and what's she's doing. Think: 'How does the setting change the way the character might say or do something?'"

- "Today I want to teach you that when you get together with your reading partner, you might want to retell the important events to make sure that the book is making sense to you. You can use the cover, title, and pictures to say what happened in the story."

- "Readers can help their partner retell by asking them questions. They can ask questions such as 'Who is in the story?' or 'What did she do?' or 'What happened to her?'"

Use this list as a menu of possibilities, selecting only the teaching points that meet the needs of your students. Use your assessment data (running records, conferring and small-group notes, observations, responses to read-alouds, and other information) to decide on a plan that is tailored to the needs of your class. These teaching points may be used as whole-class minilessons, mid-workshop teaching, or for conferences and small-group work. You need not use every teaching point. See the unit overview for guidelines on how much time to spend in each bend.

- "Sometimes readers have trouble retelling. When this happens, they should go back to the last place where everything made sense and reread from there, paying closer attention to what is happening."

- "Readers can also discuss what they noticed about the characters in their books. Just as you did on your own, you can work with a partner to look at characters' facial expressions, gestures, and actions to learn about them. You might talk about how characters are feeling at the beginning, middle, and end of a book as well as what the characters are saying (plus what they *don't* say)."

- "Sometimes the book does not come right out and tell you what the characters are thinking. Sometimes you have to figure it out on your own! To show what you think your characters are thinking, you can add speech bubbles or thought bubbles on Post-its, right onto the pages of your book."

BEND II: PARTNERS PRETEND THEY ARE CHARACTERS AND PERFORM BOOKS IN CLUBS TO BECOME CHARACTER EXPERTS

- "Today I want to teach you that one way that readers get to know the characters in their books really well is to become those characters as they read. Readers walk in the shoes of their characters, noticing when they are feeling a certain way, and then bring those feelings into their voices and gestures as they are reading and acting out the story."

- "Today I want to teach you how partners can act out scenes from texts together. One partner can be the character and the other can be the narrator of the story. The narrator reads the text that is not a 'talking part' and the other partner acts out what the character is doing, thinking, and saying."

- "Today, I want to teach you that when you and your partner are acting out books, and you come to a part where a character doesn't say anything, you can think, 'Hmm, . . . What might the character say in this part?' and then look closely at the pictures to help you imagine those words."

- "Sometimes readers work with other readers in book clubs. You can work with the readers in your club to get to know the characters in your books so well that you can make them your own. As you read and reread your books together, be sure to look at both the *words* and the *pictures*, and pay *close* attention to what the character does and says."

- "Readers, today I want to remind you that rereading can help you make your story come alive. You can read the first time just to figure out what's happening, but then you can reread again and again to make your reading smoother, and more expressive. When you reread you might try:
  - making the text sound smooth (scooping up the words into phrases instead of word by word)
  - making your voice sound like the character's
  - reading like a professional storyteller, with props and gestures and sound effects
  - 'popping out' important parts."

- "Today, I want to teach you that readers try out different ways to sound and act like their characters, and then decide on a way that best matches the clues the text provides. When readers perform their books, they can perform them a few times, but in different ways. Club members can ask themselves, 'What could we do differently?' They might try changing the characters' voices or even their feelings, until they find the best fit for the story."

- "Today I want to teach you that one thing readers do is act out scenes that are beyond what's on the pages; they act out what might come after the last page of the book. At the end of a story, you can use what you know about the character to make a good prediction about what might happen next, even though the story is over."

- "Today, I want to teach you that club members can share their different ideas about how a book might be performed, and be ready to explain their thinking, knowing that there isn't one 'Right Way.'"

BEND III: GIVING THE GIFT OF READING

- "Today, I want to teach you that you can give the gift of reading! You can think about the people you care about and which stories they would love to hear from you. You can decide what you will perform, how you will perform it, and who will be your audience."

- "Readers, it is up to you to decide which version of your book is the one you want to perform for the celebration. One way to do this is to revisit your book closely, seeing it first one way, then another, and then performing it each of these different ways. Then figure out which way you like best!"

- "Readers, each of your clubs has a goal to work on. You can help each other by reminding each other to work on your goals. When you get together in your club, you should:
  - Decide who will go first.
  - Announce your goal and read a book to your club.
  - Ask the reader questions.
  - Give the reader little tips.
  - Switch roles."

- "Today I want to teach you that when you are presenting your gift reading, you need to make sure that it is as beautiful as possible. Sometimes, though, it will not be perfect. You will mess up. But, that's okay because you can use rereading to fix it. Your listener will understand. Messing up happens to everyone. You will just need to say, 'Oops, let me try that again,' then reread that whole sentence or page."

- "Today I want to teach you that if you are stuck on a word, you can back up and get a running start toward that word. Fixing up your reading all by yourself is one of the most important signs that you are growing as a reader."

- "Today, I want to teach you that as performers get ready to share the gift of reading through a performance, they have decisions to make: will they use the exact words of the book or make up their own? How will they act out the characters? Performers try out different ways to figure out how to share their book with an audience!"

- "Readers, you can also plan for places to stop and talk about your book with your guest. You can use Post-its to mark places where you'll stop reading and talk about the book. You might mark the places where you want to:

  - Point out details in the pictures.

  - Make sound effects or facial expressions.

  - Read a page more than once.

  - Stop to say what you are thinking.

  - Ask your listener to say what he or she is thinking, too."

Kindergarten, First Grade, or Second Grade

Word Detectives Use All They Know to Solve Words

RATIONALE/INTRODUCTION

This unit has been designed to support your children's word-solving skills in several ways. First, it provides an opportunity to revisit the strategy work children already know— but may have forgotten—particularly around the use of meaning, structure, and visual cues. Second, it provides an opportunity for you to teach children some more efficient word-solving strategies that will help them read more challenging books. This is critically important work at this stage because when children read books above level D, they need word-solving strategies that leverage their burgeoning phonics knowledge. Third, your young readers will work on fluency, acting as reading detectives, searching for punctuation clues to help make their reading voices smooth like talk.

As you make plans for this unit, then, think about what many of your children are doing now when they encounter hard words in books. Think about the relationship between writing, reading, and phonics. Think about how you will support this work in all components of the literacy block and beyond, not only during reading workshop. The most important goal, of course, will be to make sure your readers are *active* problem solvers—word detectives who try several strategies whenever they come across mysterious or unknown words. This is the hardest work most new readers will do.

This unit is designed for classrooms where a large number of the children are moving into reading levels E, F, and G. This may be appropriate at the very end of kindergarten in a few instances. However, most kindergartners would probably benefit more from the "Readers Are Resourceful: Tackling Hard Words and Tricky Parts in Books" unit (found in this book). That is also a word-solving unit, but geared more toward emergent and beginning readers who are moving into reading levels A, B, C, and D.

If you teach first grade and your students are mostly reading at levels E, F, and G, and you find that they need additional support with print strategies at the start of the year, then you may want to teach this unit following *Building Good Reading Habits* (Unit 1), before diving into *Learning About the World: Reading Nonfiction* (Unit 2). This will allow you to launch your school year with Unit 1, focusing on routines and stamina, and then this unit will give kids the tools and strategies they need to tackle new and unfamiliar words before you teach your first nonfiction reading unit.

For some classrooms of second-graders, this unit might provide the extra support needed with word-attack skills, especially if a large number of your group are reading well below the benchmark for the grade. If you find that a group of your second-graders are reading at F/G during *Bigger Books Mean Amping Up Reading Power* (Unit 3), then you may want to teach this unit as an extension—either by teaching it in its entirety, or selecting particular bends and adding them to Unit 3.

ASSESSMENT

Your running records, spelling inventories, and high-frequency word assessments will be powerful sources of information for you to use as your guide for planning for this unit. As you look across the kinds of miscues students make, you'll want to make note of patterns that emerge.

As you read running records, ask yourself:

- What are my students doing (and not doing) when they encounter trouble?
- Do they make attempts?
- Do they check their attempts?
- Do they make multiple attempts?
- What sources of information do they use?
- Do they use meaning, structure, and visual information equally, or do they lean more heavily on one information source?
- How effectively do they use sources of information?
- Are there signs that my students are self-monitoring (rereading, pausing, searching the page for clues)?
- Do my students understand what they have read?

You may notice that a child often uses visual information, but only attends to the beginning of words, often leaving off the endings, interfering with the structure of the sentence. Although she clearly is using visual information, she is not yet using it effectively. As you study the data, you will be looking for patterns in individual children's reading as well as across your whole class. This will help you to set up some initial small groups, as well as shape the teaching you will do in the unit.

When you do running records, whether you are just looking on as a child reads his just-right book, or you have brought a specific book to him, it is important that you see what happens when he reads a book at a level that is a bit hard—the strategies he uses and does not yet use become easier to identify. In other words, when a reader is stretched a little, what he still needs to be taught becomes more obvious. You will be able to see whether a child relies especially on print, on the meaning of the story, or on the syntax of sentences to cope with difficult books.

If you have not yet administered a spelling inventory or a high-frequency word list assessment, you will want to be sure that you do one for each student. These assessments will give you important insight into what each student knows about how words work.

A spelling inventory will help you plan which spelling patterns your kids might call upon to help them solve unfamiliar words. For example, if your students overall know a lot about spelling common word endings (-*ing*, -*ly*, -*er*, -*ed*), then it will make sense that they could use familiar word endings to help them solve tricky words when they read. On the other hand, if your spelling inventories reveal that your students don't know much yet about spelling word endings, you will want to plan to teach that during your word work time, and will probably teach a different strategy during reading workshop. You can use an assessment like the *Words Their Way Spelling Inventories* or the *Developmental Spelling Assessment* to get the information you need to guide your instruction around specific word-solving strategies that involve spelling patterns, while in this unit.

You'll also want to check to see which high-frequency words most of you students do know (and which they still need to learn). This will let you know what words you can work on during word study and how students are building more automaticity in reading words in a snap. You can find assessments for reading high-frequency words from a number of sources, including the TCRWP website (http://readingandwritingproject.org/resources/assessments/running-records, search term "Reading and Writing Project high-frequency words"). Look across your class and build lists of words to work on this month. Also plan to pick a few words a week that differ from the words you place on the word wall, for small groups of students to work on, to help you strategically work on individual needs. In this unit, you will be teaching kids to use their knowledge of high-frequency words in a number of ways.

A SUMMARY OF THE BENDS IN THE ROAD FOR THIS UNIT

Essential Question: How can I use all the strategies that I know in ways that let me understand and figure out words in the books that I read?

- **Bend I: Detectives Work Hard to Solve Tricky Words**

  How do I get better at using strategies to figure out hard and new words while I am reading?

- **Bend II: Detectives Have Many Different Ways to Solve Words: Using Knowledge about Letters, Sounds, Patterns, and Snap Words to Read**

  How can I use what I know about how letters and sounds work to solve tricky words in my books?

- **Bend III: Rereading to Make Our Reading Sound Like Talking**

  What are ways I can reread my books to make my reading voice smoother, so that it sounds like talking?

In Bend I (Detectives Work Hard to Solve Tricky Words), you will rally your students to be the best word detectives they can be so that they can tackle any "bumps in the road." You'll begin by teaching children word-solving strategies that involve knowledge of a book's meaning: previewing the book, previewing the page, anticipating how a page will go before reading it, and relying on their understanding of the whole of the book in order to problem solve words. Next, you'll shift children's focus to word solving by relying on knowledge of language structure—that is, anticipating the *kinds* of words that come next as they read. While they won't need to identify nouns and verbs, children will think about what would sound right in a book. You will also teach students how to check on their own reading by asking themselves questions as they read. Does it make sense? Does this look right at the beginning and end? It should take you just over a week to get through this bend.

In Bend II (Detectives Have Many Different Ways to Solve Words: Using Knowledge about Letters, Sounds, Patterns, and Snap Words to Read), you'll shift to focus more on the integration of visual information in reading process work. You'll spend just over a week teaching students multiple strategies for problem solving words. This will include using knowledge of word parts and known words, including high-frequency words. Much of the instruction in this bend will be focused on partner reading. You will show students how to use what they know about problem solving words to coach their partners, and suggest prompts they can use so that they are supporting the reader without doing all the correcting for them. You'll conclude this bend by teaching partners ways to work collaboratively to use all that they've been learning about being word detectives.

In Bend III (Rereading to Make Our Reading Sound Like Talking), you'll urge readers to go back to reread parts or pages to smooth out lines once they've figured out the words. You'll also help students build greater fluency and expression as they reread multiple times, thinking about the meaning of the text and the punctuation cues, using these to portray the big feeling in their reading. Partners will work together to give each other tips to make their voices sound more like talking, rereading and rehearsing to perform scenes for an audience. Plan to spend a week in Bend III.

GETTING READY

Prepare your classroom library and teach children how to fill their book baggies for this unit.

Your classroom library is your best tool for encouraging kids to find books they want to read. It is the place in your classroom where kids go to get inspired to read. This is not a genre-specific unit, meaning students can choose from fiction and informational books. In fact, you may want to encourage kids to select equal amounts of each. As you arrange the library for this unit, you will probably want to clearly designate half of the classroom library as fiction and the other half as informational, with some of the books arranged in baskets by level, and the rest organized into topics, authors, categories, and the like. You might want to display some titles along the top to spark interest in them, or create baskets of "Favorites" or "Special Books." Some teachers hold book raffles, where kids enter their names to get the chance to read popular titles or new books when they come in.

When children shop for books for this unit of study, advise them to choose ten to twelve books at their just-right level. These are books they can read with 96% accuracy, strong comprehension, and fluency. You will also want them to have several books at their instructional levels that you will select and introduce—books they can read with 90–95% accuracy, comprehension, and fluency. (No kids should be shopping for books that are too hard or frustrating.)

Make it a point to double-check kids' book baggies each time you confer or pull a small group, in addition to being present for book shopping. While children shop, you might linger close by—perhaps you'll briefly introduce a few books that you have multiple copies of, so that you can get books into kids' hands more efficiently. After a brief introduction (title, pictures, the gist of story), you might say, "Who would like to have this book in their book baggie?" Chances are, a number of kids will want any book that you have highlighted with enthusiasm. You can also tuck in book introductions across the workshop, as you confer and work with small groups, taking a few minutes here and there to highlight a few titles, read aloud the first few pages, give a brief summary of the story, or show a few key pictures, and get those books into kids' book baggies.

Partner kids strategically for the word-solving work they will practice in this unit.

Children also receive a type of book introduction when they get together to read with their reading partners. As they listen to their partner read, or read along with their partner, they are getting experience in yet another text that they might select for themselves the next time they shop. You might decide to pair some kids with a partner who reads a level up, to foster practice at the next level. On the other hand, same-level partnerships can recommend books to one another and even swap books. They can shop for the same titles, making it easier to talk about the books they've read. Figure out what works best for you and your students, as well as the selection of texts you have in your classroom library. You will want to establish these partnerships prior to the beginning of the unit, and if possible, keep the partnerships consistent for the duration of the unit.

You'll want to make sure that your readers have partner reading time following their independent reading time on a daily basis. This increases stamina and engagement for reading and provides an opportunity for readers to deepen their comprehension of the books in their baggies.

Gather and display resources from word work (phonics/spelling).

This unit connects directly to the work students have been doing as spellers. You may want to gather up any spelling charts and tools that have been introduced and display them in an easily accessible, organized area in your classroom, so that your children will know exactly where to look when they need a reminder about a spelling pattern they've recently studied. Now is a good time to be sure that your alphabet chart is displayed clearly, your word wall can be seen easily from every kid's reading spot (without having to walk around), and that any tools you may have introduced in the past are freshened up if needed: blends charts, personalized word walls, word rings, lists of "word families" you've studied, and prefixes and suffixes are common charts and tools that you may have worked on during phonics. Make these available to students for reading workshop. You might want to give each child a folder to hold these tools (if you haven't already), or make them small enough to fit easily in the book baggies.

Select read-alouds and shared-reading texts for this unit.

This is a time to aim for reading a balance of fiction and informational texts, and to also include poetry and other text types in your read-alouds and shared-reading choices. Because this unit is not genre-specific and your kids will be reading a mix of fiction and informational texts, you can use read-aloud and shared reading to demonstrate how to preview each text, figuring out if it is narrative or informational, and then make a plan for how you will read it differently depending on the genre. (With poetry, you can show kids how to preview the text thinking, "Is this *mostly* like a story, or more like information?")

With stories, you will want to pay close attention to character feelings and how they change. You'll stop and think often about what is happening, and what the lessons the character (and the readers) might be learning. In informational texts you'll want to stop often to think and talk about the main ideas and key details, asking, "What is this mostly about?" You'll want to emphasize stopping and thinking after each section to summarize the main points, and rereading often to figure out how all the separate parts of the text fit together.

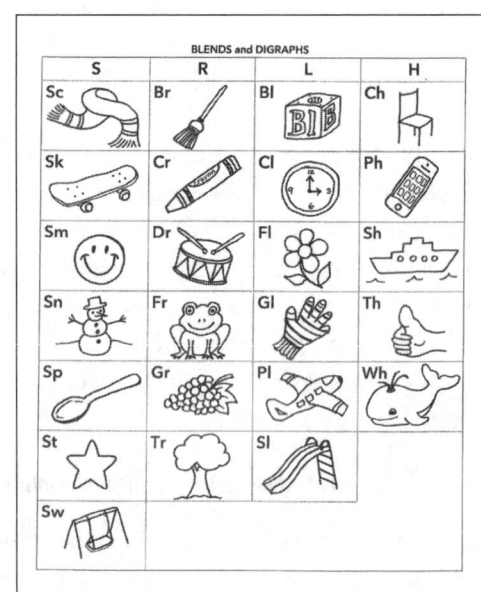

You'll probably want to select at least one or two new shared reading texts for each bend in the road of this unit, so that you can use shared-reading time to reinforce all of the strategies you'll be teaching in minilessons during reading workshop. Aim to select texts that are a level or two up from what the majority of your class reads independently so that, together, they can practice tricky words and tricky parts of the text. A text that is too easy won't provide much opportunity for authentically solving hard words.

BEND I: DETECTIVES WORK HARD TO SOLVE TRICKY WORDS

To rally your students around the goal of reading more challenging books, you could extend the metaphor of what it means to be a detective. Perhaps you will launch the unit with a mini-mystery of your own, say your glasses or your favorite coffee mug "mysteriously" disappear. You might provide a clue or two to help children solve the mystery ("I know I took a sip of my coffee and placed it on the table in the back of the classroom right before I went to pick you all up from art class. Hmm, . . ."). Perhaps you'll strategically place clues around the classroom knowing kids will come across them later in the day—a napkin stained with coffee ring. A dirty spoon. Empty sugar packets. Feel free to play up the drama and bring out your inner actor. A little drama goes a long way in raising the level of enthusiasm! Once you capture children's attention, you'll tell them that they'll be doing this same kind of detective work in their reading this month. You'll say to your class, "Readers are just like detectives! They do the exact same thing, except for instead of solving mysteries, they solve words! They open their books expecting to find hard words and then they use all their tricks to solve them!"

You might look around your classroom and observe how many students look over their books before actually turning to the first page to start reading them. Remind readers of what they probably already know about getting ready to read—"looking for clues" as to what the book will be mostly about by taking a sneak peek to get a sense of what will happen. While you may decide to teach a minilesson reviewing ways to get ready and referring back to a chart already created, you could also simply give these reminders through mid-workshop teaching points and through the read-aloud and shared-reading work outside of the reading workshop.

Teach children to use meaning, syntax, and visual information to solve words.

Once your students are in the habit of searching for meaning before they read a book, you will want to teach them that readers need to use several sources of information (just like a detective uses multiple clues) when they get to hard words—tricky spots—in their books, to solve these mystery words.

> "Today I want to teach you that when readers notice a tricky word in their book, they don't just ignore it and keep on reading. Readers *stop*. They try using one of the strategies they know to figure out the word, and then check to see if it's right. They ask themselves: 'Does it make sense? Does it sound right? Does it look right?'"

To support children in using meaning to solve unfamiliar words, you can teach children to use illustrations as clues to help them figure out those words. At levels E, F, and G, the illustrations become more complex—the picture often tells what is happening and how characters are feeling. Therefore, you might teach readers to search the illustrations like a detective, thinking about what is happening, and asking themselves, "What words might be on the page?" Then they are apt to be more successful reading the words on the page.

You will want to teach readers to shift between using strategies for reading with meaning *and* strategies for using their knowledge of language structure. For example, when a child encounters a tough word, she can think, "What kind of word would make sense *and* sound right here?" To support this kind of work, you could set your children up to "guess the covered word." Guess the covered word is a method described by Patricia Cunningham in *Month by Month Phonics*. For example, if given the sentence "The cat jumped _____ the fence," children should use what makes sense and their knowledge about language to determine that a preposition goes into that spot. You could then ask your kids to guess the word and think about the letters they expect to see in that word. Write their guesses, right and wrong, above the covered word. Then, uncover only the part of the covered word that matches the word work you know kids are using. Encourage checking and self-correction during this work.

At this point in your students' reading development, they will need to rely on all that they have learned about letters, sounds, and words in addition to using meaning and syntax knowledge in order to problem solve in efficient ways. One key word-solving strategy involving the use of visual information (letters, print) that will support the majority of your readers is looking for parts of words as they read rather than sounding out words letter by letter, which is the least effective strategy kids can use. Only about 45% of words in English are phonetic, so simply saying, "Sound it out" will probably not work much of the time. You will want to teach readers that when they are reading a tricky word, they can look carefully at not just the first letter, but the first *part* of the word. Read the first part, and ask yourself "What word would make sense that starts this way?" In subsequent minilessons, you'll remind students that looking closely at words is a helpful thing to do as readers.

> **"Today I want to teach you that in addition to thinking about what makes sense and what sounds right as they read, readers also look at words in a special way. Instead of looking at a word letter by letter, readers look for parts of words. They read words not letter by letter, but part by part."**

As readers read words part by part, they can draw on the phonics work they learned to do (at their respective spelling stages) during word study, to help them read books. Children who are now reading in levels E and F will also need to harness the patterns they know to help them read unknown words. Your spelling inventory data will help you to identify which patterns your students know so that you can expect them to use that knowledge as they read. For example, if kids are spelling words with digraphs and blends correctly, you will want them to use that knowledge when reading words. If they come to a word that begins with a blend or a digraph, such as *blossom*, you'll want students to read *bl* as a blend, not letter by letter. A child who reads the sentence "She did not want to stay," should be trying to see the "st" and then "ay" parts of the word, and then use those parts to read the whole word by blending them together. You will also want to teach students to check to see if a word looks right by doing a "slow check." Just like they say a word slowly when they are writing, they can run their finger under a word and say it slowly to check all the parts.

> **"Today I want to teach you that just like detectives always double-check their work, so do readers. When you want to check to see if a word looks right you can do a *slow check*. Just say the word slowly like you do when you are writing, and run your finger under the word. Say it slowly and check all the parts."**

As you confer with your students, and rejoice at their growing problem-solving abilities, you may be tempted to say things like "Good job" and "That's right" each time they read a word correctly. Students themselves reinforce this reaction by looking to us for help or reassurance when they stop at a word or are confused. We caution you to resist the urge to tell a child when a word is right, because your most important reading goal is to get kids to do their own monitoring. When we teach students how to self-monitor we support their independence. If we always tell them when a word is right or wrong, they simply learn to depend on others, not themselves, in the face of challenge. Instead of depending on us to confirm, you will want to ask them, "Were you right?" so that they will self-assess and realize that the strategy they have employed is successful. Our goal as teachers is to set our students up to reach the higher-level, independent strategizing work.

Channel children to fix words when they don't sound like the language the book is using.

We have found it is essential that your students learn how to check their own reading. It is extremely important that they learn to stop when something doesn't make sense in a story, or when something doesn't sound or look correct. They can ask themselves questions like, "Does this go with the story? Does this sound like a book?" As children read, call out little prompts to remind them to do this work. Some students will know exactly what to do when you say "Check it." Others will need a little more prompting such as, "You said 'Mom *want* in the car.' Does that sound right?" After fixing a word, students should reread the sentence to make sure that this time it does sound right. Be on the lookout in your classroom for kids who are stopping and finding parts that sound wrong or that just don't make sense. Celebrate them—shout out the powerful work they are doing during mid-workshop teaching. Tell the rest of the class how they worked hard to figure something out in a share session. Encourage kids to bring difficulties that they fixed up or need more help in fixing to their partners.

Readers who are monitoring for sense more consistently are ones who you'll see occasionally pausing or stopping after reading a tricky word, rereading, asking their partner for help during partner reading, or searching for more information. You'll want to celebrate this and then move into teaching ways to self-correct as they read. As readers begin to self-correct, they will often read an entire sentence before going back to fix up a word. As they become stronger with this aspect of the reading process, they will self-correct closer to the error.

As you analyze your running records, notice whether students are self-correcting as they read, and look to see that students are monitoring consistently rather than sparingly. You may notice that your students are consistently searching for meaning, structure, and visual information but never monitoring and correcting. If this is the case, you might decide to spend more time on this during shared reading as you continue on to the next bend. In your shared reading you can continue modeling how readers reread, pause to think, and notice when things aren't quite right. You might also decide to extend this bend by a day or two to emphasize self-monitoring and correcting.

BEND II: DETECTIVES HAVE MANY DIFFERENT WAYS TO SOLVE WORDS: USING KNOWLEDGE ABOUT LETTERS, SOUNDS, PATTERNS, AND SNAP WORDS TO READ

Build children's automaticity for "snap" words.

As you move into the second bend, your instructional focus will shift from using meaning and syntax, to homing in on the print. You'll teach kids a number of strategies for looking very closely at words to solve them. Keep in mind that while the main instruction in this part of the unit is focused on the visual information or word parts, it is critical that you are continuing using meaning and syntax as you model so that readers are seeing how you orchestrate multiple sources of information.

Of course, as children tackle hard words, you'll also want to make sure that they do not need to work hard to tackle *every* word. More than half the words that readers at this age encounter are the same thirty-six words! Remember that many children had more than twenty-five words under their belt by the time they left kindergarten. Lots of other words they encounter are ones they should know with automaticity. It is important that by this time your children all have a substantial repertoire of words they know "in a snap." These words will be a great help as they read. This unit is a good time to rally children's enthusiasm for extending their high-frequency sight vocabularies.

You may want to encourage students to do a quick warm-up routine before they begin independent reading each day. You might suggest that just as detectives often review all the clues to a mystery to get their minds focused, readers also can review what they know before they start reading. They might read all the "snap words" on the class word wall, or from a personal word wall in their book baggies, to rev up their minds and prepare for the words they're likely to find in their leveled books.

> **"Just as detectives often review all the clues to a mystery to get their minds focused, readers can also review what they know before they start reading. One way to do this is by reading the word wall before you start to read your book so that these words are fresh on your mind and you can read them in a snap."**

Some of your students may need help with high-frequency words. Perhaps you'll give each of these children word rings, made with index cards held together by a ring or string, holding the words you have been teaching a particular child to read in a snap. Perhaps one child will have fifteen words on that word ring, and another child will have twenty-five on their ring. Over time, words they know perfectly can be removed so as to focus on the words they almost know. Other children may benefit from having known and unknown words on the word ring to reinforce the known words and build confidence. Sometimes readers know these words in isolation or in the context of the word wall, but have difficulty recognizing these words automatically while reading.

It is important to remember that putting words on the word wall or word ring is not enough. The words need to be introduced and explicitly taught. Patricia Cunningham, in *Month by Month Phonics for First Grade*, recommends that when placing a word on the word wall the procedure should be: kids glue their eyes to the word (visual), cheer for the word (auditory), and then write the word (kinesthetic). If you add five words a week, this process should take no more than five minutes a day and will be time very well spent.

Children who need special help with high-frequency words could also play games to practice reading these words. One child can sit with another, looking at the word wall, and the first can say, "I spy a word that is . . ." and then give hints until the other child guesses the selected word. You can simply give these children a pointer and ask them to take time every day to read the words on the word wall. Some teachers try to make this fun by suggesting children take on different voices each time they reread the word wall.

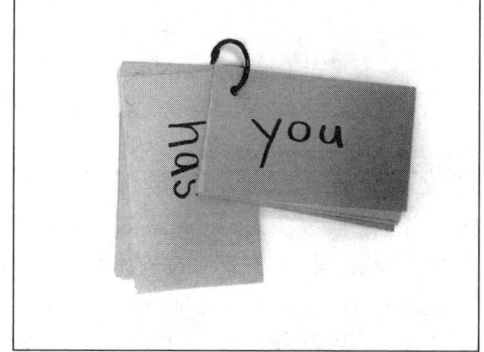

A word ring like this is a helpful tool for young readers who are working on mastering high-frequency words. One or two words are introduced at a time and added to the ring so the child will have a personal resource.

One partner can say to the other, "Read the word wall in a witch's voice," or "Read the word wall like a cat by meowing the words." These are silly instructions, but the point is for these words to become automatic for children, and they will benefit from repeated practice. Of course, the best way for children to learn sight vocabulary words is by seeing those words again and again in real books at their just-right level, which is the essential thing they do during reading workshop.

The other important thing about increasing students' high-frequency word vocabulary is that these words give students a running start that often provides the necessary momentum to figure out tricky parts in their books. For example, if a child is reading *Walking in the Spring* by Beverley Randell and encounters the sentence, "If you go for a walk down by a river, look for ducklings," she is likely to be able to read, "If you go for a walk down by a river," because most of those words are in her high-frequency word vocabulary.

Teach students that high-frequency words are like clues to a mystery or pieces of a puzzle. You can use the clues you do know to figure out the mystery, or what isn't there. In the connection part of a minilesson, you could show students a partially finished jigsaw puzzle, and have them guess what the missing pieces probably show. Then, as you snap in the missing pieces, highlight that they used the pieces they knew as clues to figure out what would make sense, and what would fit in the empty spots. Then, in the teaching part of your minilesson, you can go on to demonstrate reading a line or two from an unfamiliar big book, using high-frequency words as clues to figure out unknown words. With some of the "mystery words" covered with Post-its, you can demonstrate how you use the words you know to make a guess at what would make sense.

You'll also show students how they can use parts of high-frequency words to help them read new words. The words *she* and *can*, for example, have the "sh" digraph and the "an" spelling pattern that are in so many other words. These strategies for using visual information, such as parts of words and making connections between words, are used most successfully by readers reading above level D.

Teach students to use what they know from word work (spelling/phonics) to solve unfamiliar words.

During word work (phonics) time, you will likely be studying spelling patterns, including common word endings (*-ed*, *-er*, *-ly*, *-ing* are examples), and long and short vowel patterns through word sorts, word games, and other activities. In writing workshop you'll be encouraging students to use everything they know about spelling to write words as best they can. During activities like shared reading, shared writing, and interactive writing, students will see you model the use of all the spelling patterns they've been studying in a meaningful context. In this bend, you will also teach students to use that knowledge to read unfamiliar words in books.

As students move into higher reading levels, they will be reading longer words with more syllables. For children moving from the reading levels A–D into reading levels E, F, and G, there won't always be such clear picture support for the words, and sometimes they will need to be able to decode simple two-syllable words. They'll need to be able to break the words into familiar spelling patterns. That means being able to see that a word like *always* can be broken into parts, /al/ways/.

Once students understand that there are patterns to how words work, as readers, they can run their finger underneath the word from left to right, looking for where they see a pattern they know. Encourage kids not to get too picky about where to split a word—try it out more than one way! Help them to see that when they split a word apart into pieces, it's much easier to figure out.

You will also need to teach them how to use their knowledge of particular spelling patterns, like common word endings, as they read longer words. For instance, the word *starting* could be overwhelming, but by using the picture and knowledge of what is happening in the book as well as breaking off the ending, now having "start" and "ing" it is much easier to decode. Once they've broken the word apart, the next step is to put it back together again, saying the whole word as one. Finally, they'll need to reread to smooth out the sentence, in order to be sure that the word sounds right and makes sense for the book. After teaching this through shared reading, you can coach kids to transfer this learning and apply this strategy when they come to a tricky word in their own independent reading.

Another strategy to teach is "word analogy," that is, using familiar parts of known words as tools to figure out unfamiliar words. For example, in some phonics programs *cat* becomes the anchor word for -*at* words, and *sit* becomes the anchor word for -*it* words. The goal of teaching anchor words is to be able to say, "If I know *cat* then I know *sat*, and *rat*, and *mat*, and *bat*." Once children have mastered the spelling of an anchor word, they can use it for reading and writing many new words. These are words that you might have on display in your classroom, or that children might have on index cards or mini-charts as reminders. You could say to students: "Today I want to teach you that you can use parts of words you know to help you figure out new words. When you come to a tricky word, stop, and ask yourself, 'Does part of this look like a word I know?' Read or say the word you know, then go back to the tricky word to figure out the part that is the same."

In a minilesson, you can demonstrate this by using a big book to model reading, and then becoming stuck on a word like *sled*. "Yikes! I don't know that word!" you'll pretend. "Hmm, . . . Does this look like a word I know?" Then point to a chart listing familiar anchor words from your phonics instruction (*cat*, *sit*, and *bed*, might be a few words on that list). Students will likely immediately call out "bed!" But, you will want to demonstrate deliberate thinking, pointing to each of the anchor words, one at a time to decide, because that is what children will need to do on their own, if an anchor word doesn't immediately pop out at them. When you land on *bed* you'll say, "Aha! Bed! I see a part that looks the same. So . . . if this word is /b/ed/ (emphasize the sound the -*ed* makes), then this new word must be . . . /sl/ed/. Did you see how I used part of a word I already know to help me figure out a new word?"

Of course, some tricky words will have whole words inside them that are familiar to children. Words like *sand*, *something*, and *called* can all be solved by looking inside the word for other words. Of course, it's important to be flexible with a strategy like this one. Think of words like *whole* (who), or *another* (a not her). There are many times where finding a word inside another word will not be so helpful, and so kids will simply need to be flexible and try another strategy instead.

The important thing here is to demonstrate how readers use more than one strategy at once to tackle the hard words and tricky parts of books. It is essential that your students have the mind-set and the tools to tackle tricky words with vigor and independence in all components of the day, transferring these skills from one to another. This is intellectually demanding work for young readers.

> **"One way that readers are just like detectives is that when there is a mystery to solve, they don't just try one way to solve it, and then give up if that one way doesn't work. They keep trying and trying different ways until something makes sense."**

You will probably want to create an anchor chart that threads across the unit, so that as you teach each new strategy, children have a visual reminder of all the strategies they can choose from. The chart can grow over these few weeks, and can continue to grow even across the school year. You'll perhaps create a new version of it when children no longer need reminders for strategies that they have mastered and are using automatically.

Differentiate instruction to support readers moving up text levels.

To differentiate your minilessons, think about ways in which you can support diverse readers during the active engagement. For instance, instead of having everyone practice the strategy in a shared text, you might say, "Try this in your just-right book." Some teachers also find it helps to establish a seating chart that groups children, giving each cluster an appropriate book with which to work during the active engagements. Both shared reading and read-aloud will also provide opportunities for the class as a whole to do more close-in, scaffolded work with grade-level books.

This unit is geared toward a classroom of children who are mostly reading around levels E, F, and G. The handful of students who are not reading these levels will need tailored instruction through one-on-one conferring, guided reading, shared reading, and small-group strategy lessons to help them move along. When you meet with these children you will want to find ways to explicitly name which of the whole-class strategies will be helpful, and which will not. For example, it will not be helpful for level A/B readers to focus on dividing words into syllables or using a word-analogy strategy—their attention is much better directed toward the pictures and the meaning, holding on to the pattern in the book, and pointing crisply under the first letter of each word. Some teachers routinely meet with a small group immediately following the minilessons to clarify how that day's teaching does or does not apply to that group's work as readers. You might find it helpful to create individualized charts for these readers, and to color-code the charts you do have on display for the class so that you can direct each reader to the appropriate ones.

If you have emergent readers who are on the cusp of conventional reading (levels A, B, C), aim to lead many guided reading sessions with them. If possible, work with the most vulnerable children several times a week in small groups. During guided reading sessions, choose books the children will be able to read easily with just a little support; give them a book introduction and then let them each read the book alone (yet alongside each other) while you lean in to coach one child's reading and then the next. Keep in mind that these beginning readers will be reading just-right books with relatively supportive illustrations accompanying the book. While much of your word-solving instruction will focus on using pictures to help them attend to meaning, make sure these readers also attend to print. These students may only be able to use beginning sounds and ending sounds. If your children have demonstrated a solid grasp of initial and final sounds on the spelling inventory, this would lead you to teach them that when they come to a hard word, they should look at the picture and the first sound of the word, thinking of words they know that look and sound like that.

You might demonstrate this by looking, for example, at the sentence, "I like to eat popcorn." Cover most of the word *popcorn* with just the letter *p* showing at the beginning and the letter *n* at the end of the word. Say, "I'm looking at the first letter of this word. /P/. That is the first letter sound of the word I've read. /P/. Let's see. What could it be? It should be something that I eat. Play dough? Pizza? Popcorn? Let's check the picture! I see popcorn. Let's say *popcorn* and think about what we hear at the end. Now let's check the ending part." Pointing to the *n* you might say, "What does that sound make?" Then show children how they can think about their guesses to pick the one that makes sense, sounds right, and looks right. Once you have introduced these books in guided reading, you will want to make sure that the books are in the book baggies so kids can practice the strategies you have taught them and to reread the books with fluency.

You may want to do some small-group strategy lessons with your stronger readers in which you teach reading strategies appropriate to their level. Take a close look at the books they are reading and determine any challenges the books present. Observe what children need to work on and then choose prompts that scaffold them toward independence. Remember that at higher levels, readers will encounter challenging words, but they will also struggle at times to make meaning from books. When a group of children in your room face the latter challenge, you could pull them into a small group and use a shared book to teach them how to hold on to more text across pages. As you read across one or more pages, stop and ask the children to think about what they just read and describe this in a simple sentence. For example, a child who is reading the book *Walking in the Spring* by Beverley Randell might stop at the end of the first few pages and say, "This is a book that is about a family seeing flowers when they go for a walk." However, if you ask her to think about the whole book, the title, and how the pages go together, she is more likely to come up with a summary that encompasses the meaning of the whole story, like, "This is a book about a family that sees many things they never saw before because it's spring and the flowers are coming out and baby animals are born on the farm." This kind of close reading instruction will support children to retell in more sophisticated ways as they move into more complex books. This work will likely be the focus of some of your small groups with readers who are moving up levels quickly. Of course, you will want to be sure that you help these advancing readers be able to talk about what the book is mostly about and key details of their books, before you continually add more complex books to their reading diets.

BEND III: REREADING TO MAKE OUR READING SOUND LIKE TALKING

Your readers now have a growing repertoire of strategies for problem solving words and are becoming more independent as they more consistently self-monitor and self-correct using their strategies. During partner reading time, you've probably noticed readers helping each other in many ways. Often this may look like one partner correcting a word for the other partner. This is a great time to lift the level of this work by having readers take more responsibility for prompting their partners to problem solve, monitor, and correct their reading.

Spotlight the importance of rereading for smoothness.

As children encounter tricky parts and work through them, teach them how to go back and reread until the book goes smoothly. You might model with a sentence or two on a chart. Demonstrate how a reader gets to a tricky part, uses all she knows to figure out the word(s), and then goes back to read it smoothly. Teach children that when we read smoothly, instead of haltingly or v-e-r-y s-l-o-w-l-y, we are more likely to understand what we are reading. It's important to let partners know that as they read a book over and over again across the week, their voices should become smoother and smoother until they no longer stumble on tricky parts and they get to a comfortable-to-listen-to speed. If by the end of the week, a book doesn't feel smooth to a child, he should plan to keep the book in his baggie for another week. This is another great way that partners can support each other's growth, cheering each other on as words get smoother or supporting each other to make a decision to hold on to the book. In other words, just as reading out loud to someone else can help a writer make her writing smoother, reading a book out loud to a partner can help a reader make his reading smoother.

> **"Today I want to teach you that after readers have read once to fix up the tricky words, they can reread to make their reading sound smooth. You read, fix it, and read again, putting it all back together."**

Often the act of rereading a sentence provides readers with an opportunity to consider the meaning and syntax again before they do the visual work of looking at the parts of the words. You may say to kids, "Sometimes when we read, we *know* all the words, but we forget to think, 'What is this part saying?' or 'What does this *really* mean?' Readers often reread as they are reading to check in with themselves and make sure that they know what is happening or what the book is saying."

> **"Readers, it is so important to reread! Today I want to teach you that when readers reread, they think even *more* about what is happening. They sometimes ask themselves, 'What is this part saying?' or 'What does this really *mean*?' That way, they're always thinking about the book."**

Teach students to attend closely to punctuation as they reread, using it as a cue to reflect the intended tone of the text, matching their voices. Partnerships can work together to practice these strategies for reading (and rereading) with more fluency and expression. Teach partners to listen closely to one another as they read aloud, giving each other tips to make their reading voices even smoother, to sound more like talking.

Teach children specific strategies for reading fluently and making new words part of their reading repertoire.

Now that you've introduced the big picture, reading smoothly, you might want to teach more targeted strategies for reading fluently. Keep in mind that reading fluently is multidimensional, having to do with various combinations of the appropriate pace or reading rate (including automaticity and accuracy), phrasing (smoothness, grouping words, pausing where appropriate), and prosody (expression, tone, feeling).

As children move into the new books in their baggies that they've selected for the week, they will encounter new words to solve. You can teach them that when they solve a new word, one strategy is to say that new word several times to yourself, reread the sentence it was in, and even try saying it in a new sentence, perhaps telling your partner what the new word means, or pointing to the picture and saying how the new word fits with what is happening. By repeating the new word several times, both in and out of context, readers are more likely to recognize it automatically when they encounter it again, either later on in the same book or when they reread the book.

Another strategy for helping kids hang on to new words they have worked hard to solve is to write them down on a Post-it. The physical act of writing is often helpful for committing a word to memory, so that they next time the child is faced with that same word, she won't have to start all over again, solving it from scratch. On her next read, that word can be read just as smoothly as any other word.

> **"Readers, today I want to teach you that when I've worked hard to figure out a new word, I want to remember it the next time I see it—so I don't have to start all over again to figure it out! Sometimes I say the word three times to myself, and use it in a few sentences. Sometimes I talk about the word with my partner. And then other times, I write the word down. This way, when I come across that word again I'll be able to read it just as smoothly as any other word I know. You can pick the strategies that work best for you."**

Now that kids are reading longer books than ever before, there is a good chance there may be more lines of print on a page than they have been used to. A good strategy, then, is to teach kids to scoop up words in phrases, grouping the words that "go together." In a minilesson, you can demonstrate how on a first read, you might be reading one. word. at. a. time. But then, on a reread, you can group the words into three- and four-word phrases that make sense. As an active engagement, you might cut apart a sentence strip, and ask children to come up to a pocket chart to move words closer together or further apart to show which words would sound right together as phrases. You can highlight how there may not be just one way to read a sentence, and that readers are flexible, trying it one way and then another to make their reading sound right.

Sometimes readers are in the habit of stopping too often because they haven't practiced scanning all the way to the end of a line or the end of a page. Pushing oneself to read *all the way* to the end of the sentence (or page in the earlier levels) is one way to smooth out your reading. Teach children that after looking at the picture to think about what the page will probably be about, they can then scan the print before they read to get a sense of how much text they are going to read. They can even run their finger under the print and physically point to the spot in the text they plan to read smoothly to. This encourages kids to look beyond one-word-at-a-time reading, while at the same time encourages them to read more smoothly.

Children can also scan the print for end punctuation, quotation marks, and other clues (bold words, all caps) that will help them prepare for reading the print smoothly when they get to those places. Teach kids that scanning ahead is something that readers do all the time. You might even tell them about the famous studies that researchers have done where they track eye movements while grown-ups are reading—turns out grown-ups don't usually look at words one at a time, left to right! Their eyes look over the whole page while they read, searching for all kinds of clues.

Chances are, the books your children are reading still have quite a few features that help children read them smoothly. Many books at these levels rhyme. Many still have patterns of some kind, too. Lots of books are written in a singsongy or predictable way that helps students read them fluently. Teach kids that as they reread their books, they might listen for these things, the rhyme, the pattern, or rhythm. "Listen for the song inside the text," you might say, "then reread and practice making your voice match how the book wants to be read."

CELEBRATION

You launched this unit with a mystery for kids to solve. Whether it was a missing coffee mug or a pair of reading glasses, your kids searched the classroom for clues to help you solve the mystery. On that day, you invited your students to become detectives. Today, you'll celebrate that they've not only become detectives in the classroom, but they've also become word detectives. They approach unfamiliar words with a willingness to search for clues, solve problems, and puzzle things out. Perhaps you'll celebrate this work by inviting kids to join you in solving one last big mystery. You could pass out "mystery envelopes" containing riddles or clues for partners to solve together—each message providing clues to one mystery word. "I am a word wall word that starts with 't' and I mean more than one," might be a clue to the word "two." Then when all the words have been solved, the class can work together to put the words in order to form a special message to kids. Perhaps the message will announce that a special surprise guest reader will now read a favorite story to them, or that you have a brand-new big book to read together. Use your imagination and your knowledge of your kids' interests to decide on a celebration of reading that will be meaningful for your class.

BEND I: DETECTIVES WORK HARD TO SOLVE TRICKY WORDS

- "Today I want to teach you that readers are like detectives. Detectives work hard to solve mysteries—and readers work hard to solve words and understand their books. They open their books expecting to find hard words and then they use all their tricks to solve them!"

- "Today I want to teach you that when readers notice a tricky word in their book, they don't just ignore it and keep on reading. Readers *stop*. They try using one of the strategies they know to figure out the word, and then check to see if it's right. They ask themselves: 'Does it make sense? Does it sound right? Does it look right?'"

- "Today I want to teach you that readers do so much more than simply check the picture when they get to a tricky word. Readers search the pictures like a detective and think about what is happening in the story, then they ask themselves, 'What words might be on the page?'"

- "One thing readers do when they are stuck on a tricky word is they stop and think, 'What would make sense *and* sound right in a sentence?' Then they can play 'Guess the Covered Word' to figure out the word.

  1. Cover the word, and make a guess that makes sense.

  2. Make sure the word sounds right in a sentence.

  3. Write the word—what letters do you expect to see?

  4. Check the first letter, the last letter, and look all the way through the word to double-check your guess."

- "Today I want to teach you that in addition to thinking about what makes sense and what sounds right as they read, readers also look at words in a special way. Instead of looking at a word letter by letter, readers look for parts of words. They read words not letter by letter, but part by part."

- "Today I want to teach you that just like detectives always double-check their work, so do readers. When you want to check to see if a word looks right you can do a *slow check*. Just say the word slowly like you do when you are writing, and run your finger under the word. Say it slowly and check all the parts."

- "Today I want to teach you that you can help your partner when reading books together. For example, you can say things like, 'Stop! Something isn't right.' 'Fix it!' 'Try that again.' You can also check the charts to remind you of other things to say. And, you can also be your own partner, reminding yourself to stop when something doesn't make sense, and use a strategy to fix it."

Use this list as a menu of possibilities, selecting only the teaching points that meet the needs of your students. Use your assessment data (running records, conferring and small-group notes, observations, responses to read-alouds, and other information) to decide on a plan that is tailored to the needs of your class. These teaching points may be used as whole-class mini-lessons, mid-workshop teaching points, or for conferences and small-group work. You need not use every teaching point. See the unit overview for guidelines on how much time to spend in each bend.

BEND II: DETECTIVES HAVE MANY DIFFERENT WAYS TO SOLVE WORDS: USING KNOWLEDGE ABOUT LETTERS, SOUNDS, PATTERNS, AND SNAP WORDS TO READ

- "Just as detectives often review all the clues to a mystery to get their minds focused, readers can also review what they know before they start reading. One way to do this is by reading the word wall before you start to read your book so that these words are fresh in your mind and you can read them in a snap."

- "Readers, today I want to teach you that snap words (high-frequency words) are like clues to a mystery or pieces of a puzzle. You can use the clues you do know to figure out the missing pieces by thinking about what would make sense."

- "Today I want to teach you that when you get to a long tricky word, don't back down! Break that word apart. One trick for doing this is to look across the word to see if there is a word ending you know. If there is, you can break the ending off, and then figure out the part that is left over. Finally, you'll need to put the pieces back together again to say the whole word in a way that makes sense and sounds right."

- "Today I want to teach you that you can use parts of words you know to help you figure out new words. When you come to a tricky word, stop, and ask yourself, 'Does part of this look like a word I know?' Read or say the word you know, then go back to the tricky word to figure out the part that is the same. For example, *bed* helps me read *sled*."

- "One way that readers are just like detectives is that when there is a mystery to solve, they don't just try one way to solve it, and then give up if that one way doesn't work. They keep trying and trying different ways until something makes sense."

BEND III: REREADING TO MAKE OUR READING SOUND LIKE TALKING

- "Today I want to teach you that after readers have read once to fix up the tricky words, they can reread to make their reading sound smooth. You read, fix it, and read again, putting it all back together."

- "Readers, it is so important to reread! Today I want to teach you that when readers reread, they think even *more* about what is happening. They sometimes ask themselves, 'What is this part saying?' or 'What does this really *mean*?' That way, they're always thinking about the book."

- "Today I want to teach you that readers pay close attention to punctuation as they read and reread. Readers use punctuation marks as clues to how to make their voice sound. Reading partners can work together, listening carefully to each other as they read aloud, and giving each other tips to make their reading voices even smoother, to sound more like talking."

- "Readers, today I want to teach you that when I've worked hard to figure out a new word, I want to remember it the next time I see it—so I don't have to start all over again to figure it out! Sometimes I say the word three times to myself and use it in a few sentences. Sometimes I talk about the word with my partner. And then other times, I write the word down. This way, when I come across that word again I'll be able to read it just as smoothly as any other word I know. You can pick the strategies that work best for you."

- "Today I want to teach you that readers 'scoop up' words in phrases, grouping the words that 'go together.' This helps make reading sound smooth, like talking. There may not be just one way to read a sentence though, so readers are flexible, trying it one way and then another to make their reading sound right."

- "Today I want to teach you that after readers check the picture to think about what might make sense for the story, they often scan the text by running their finger under the words just to see how much print they will need to read."

- "Readers can look for punctuation clues that let them know they'll need to change their voice as they read. Readers scan ahead in the reading and look for ending punctuation, quotation marks (which show someone is talking), bold words, or all capital letters."

- "Today I want to teach you that as you reread your books, listen for the rhyme, the pattern, or the rhythm. Listen for the song inside the text, then reread and practice making your voice match how the book wants to be read."

Reading Nonfiction Cover to Cover

Nonfiction Book Clubs

RATIONALE/INTRODUCTION

Nonfiction reading has come a long way. Years ago, much of what was available for kids was in the vein of encyclopedias, reference books, magazines (if you were lucky), and perhaps a slim selection of trade books on informational topics. A generation ago, nonfiction reading was not something children usually did for fun. Traditionally, these books were used as resources to skim and scan—not to read from cover to cover, and certainly not to get lost in the way one might find oneself lost in a fiction book. Fortunately for us, and for the children we teach, things have changed dramatically in recent years.

These days there are beautiful nonfiction books published at every level, full of glossy photographs and engaging writing. These books are meant to be enjoyed in their entirety, not just skimmed, and not just used as sources for the odd fact or quote. Many nonfiction books for children today contain vivid imagery, action, humor, and connections to children's lives—they are every bit as interesting as fiction. And many children, as you probably already know, actually prefer today's nonfiction over fiction and other types of reading. For these children, this is not just a unit that will make them stronger academically—this is the unit they have been waiting for!

In this unit, you will strive both to improve your students' nonfiction reading skills, and to work on their speaking and listening skills. You'll teach them how to read nonfiction, *really* read it, fully and deeply from the first page to the last. You'll help them move from simply "fact collecting," to a deeper understanding of main ideas and supporting information. Kids will be reading longer books than they ever have, and will need new strategies for hanging on to the important information (and how to let go of the not-so-important information). They will also learn to take the information provided in one book and add it to information learned in another, and another, thinking and learning about a topic across many texts, not just one.

This is a unit for children who are transitional readers, reading early chapter books or harder (around levels H–M). The unit is designed to help kids accumulate text across these long (but not too long) books. They will learn to synthesize and summarize the information into main ideas, rather than retell lists of relatively unimportant details. For a classroom comprised mostly of children reading shorter, easier books than this, the "Growing Expertise in Little Books: Nonfiction Reading" unit is perhaps a better match if you are looking for a nonfiction unit to supplement the book at your grade level.

For some first-grade classes, this unit might be a good choice if you would like to return to nonfiction reading with your first-graders near the end of the year, when the majority of your students will be reading higher levels than they were during the fall unit, *Learning About the World: Reading Nonfiction* (Unit 2). This unit provides an opportunity for your class to revisit informational reading, this time with the added feature of book clubs.

If you teach second grade and you want to extend the work your second-graders began to do in *Becoming Experts: Reading Nonfiction* (Unit 2), then this unit will provide more practice reading across texts—this time with a new spin—reading about and talking about nonfiction topics in clubs. You might add this entire unit following Unit 2, or select particular bends and insert them into that unit as extensions. Or, you might decide to teach this unit later in the year as a return to nonfiction reading, this time in the form of clubs.

ASSESSMENT

As you prepare to teach this unit, it will be helpful to have a sense of how well your class can handle nonfiction reading. You can conduct an informal pre-assessment of information reading at the start of this unit. This will set you up to track and support your students' progress on important nonfiction reading skills.

You can select an engaging nonfiction read-aloud, one that is at grade-level text complexity, and identify a few parts where kids will do some quick stop-and-jot assessments. This will reveal how they engage with the particular skills that you plan on teaching. For example, in Bend I, you'll be doing a lot of work with main ideas. In your pre-assessment you might identify a part of the book where you think the main topic is clear, and at that part in your read-aloud, ask your students to stop and jot the heading they would give that section. In order to give children more than one chance to engage with this skill, read on, but this time ask students to describe what a part is mostly about or jot down the key details and why they are important. You can then assess your students' responses and identify the next steps they need.

You can also choose places in your read-aloud to prompt for students' ideas and opinions about the text, as well as to compare and contrast what they've learned from different parts of the book. This will yield snapshots of their thinking that will help you to plan for Bends II and III. You can study students' responses and create groups based on this data. For example, some predictable responses will include students who write facts or summaries when prompted for opinions and ideas, as well as students who develop ideas that are loosely related or not at all accountable to the information in the text. There may be students whose comparisons don't make sense, and there may be students who have difficulty responding at all to the text.

If you want a more complex performance assessment and one that combines students' reading and writing, you may decide to use the Performance Assessment found in *Writing Pathways* from the Units of Study for Teaching Opinion, Information, and Narrative Writing. You can adapt the performance assessment to highlight certain standards, then analyze kids' work to determine what skills you will want to emphasize as you plan for this unit.

At the end of the unit, you may want to conduct a post-assessment. You can give the exact same assessment, reading aloud the same book, or select a new and comparable book, and then ask similar questions. By placing the student responses from this summative assessment alongside those they gave earlier in the unit, you and your students can determine how much they have grown as a result of your teaching. This information will also position you to set new goals to teach toward in the content areas as well as in your upcoming units of study in reading.

A SUMMARY OF THE BENDS IN THE ROAD FOR THIS UNIT

Essential Question: How can I gather information about a topic that interests me, comparing, contrasting, and synthesizing my own ideas and those of others (authors and the people in my club), so that my club and I can develop new ideas?

- **Bend I: Individuals Bring Their Strengths as Nonfiction Readers to Clubs**

  How can I draw on everything I know about informational reading to understand how the different parts of the books I read go together, and to assume a teaching voice and stance as I read, so that I am able to share my learning with my reading club?

- **Bend II: Nonfiction Clubs Add Their Own Ideas to What They Learn**

  How can my club and I work together to add our own thinking to the information we learn from the books we read? How can we hold meaningful conversations, make inferences, revise our thinking, and grow ideas, in the company of one another?

- **Bend III: Nonfiction Clubs Compare and Contrast Information about Topics**

  How can my club and I compare and contrast two (or perhaps more) texts on the same topic and put together this information to come up with newer, bigger thinking?

In Bend I (Individuals Bring Their Strengths as Nonfiction Readers to Clubs), you will begin by revisiting earlier teaching, reminding children of the essential habits of mind that make for proficient nonfiction reading and tackling difficulty in texts. You'll teach children strategies for previewing the text, making predictions, and to make plans for reading and rereading. You'll highlight various text structures that your students might encounter and teach strategies for how to read differently, depending on the structure of the text. You'll also support them in working together as a club, sorting books into baskets, selecting a topic together, and talking about what they are reading. Plan to spend a little over a week in Bend I.

In Bend II (Nonfiction Clubs Add Their Own Ideas to What They Learn), students will continue to learn strategies for hanging on to the information the author is aiming to teach, but will also learn to develop their own ideas about the texts. You'll spend up to two weeks teaching children to develop ideas and opinions about the information they are learning, and to refer back to the text to support their ideas.

In Bend III (Nonfiction Clubs Compare and Contrast Information about Topics), children will compare and contrast information and ideas within books, across books, and across baskets. Kids can work together with their club members to talk across books. You'll teach kids to consider both the content and the style of books as they notice similarities and differences. It will take about a week to teach the final bend in the unit.

GETTING READY

Prepare your classroom library for nonfiction book clubs for transitional readers.

As in other units, you will want to use your classroom library as a tool for providing your students with the books they need and want to read. It's helpful to think about your classroom library from a student's perspective. When a child enters the library, can she easily determine what topics her club might choose from? Once her club has decided on a topic to study and talk about together, can she find plenty of books on that topic at her just-right level? Will the other members of her book club be able to find multiple books on that topic as well?

Before launching into this unit, you will need to comb through your classroom library and likely even head to your school library to find any and all informational texts you can get your hands on. Your first step is to decide if you have enough materials to teach a unit that is designed for children to read only nonfiction for four or five weeks. Ideally, you will have enough nonfiction books so that you can create topic bins containing at least eight to ten books for each club to share. Each club will need its own basket of just-right texts to read, study, and talk about for each week of this unit. For example, you might have a bin for all the books about sharks, and another for books about pets, and another still for books about natural disasters, and another for all the books about the rain forest. Aim for more specific topics (rather than broad all-inclusive categories), if possible. The more specific the topic, the easier it will be for children to have meaningful conversations. If you do not have the resources to support at least that number of books on a topic, then you might want to consider pooling resources with your grade-level colleagues and staggering when each of you will teach this unit, so as to be able to share a "mobile" nonfiction reading club library, so to speak.

If informational books are in short supply in your classroom, you may find that you do need to make the topics rather broad in order to find books that fit: plants, ocean life, weather. If this is the case, you may want to plan ahead to read aloud to the class a book or two that fit with each topic bin. When clubs meet to talk about the topic they will all have some background knowledge and experience from the read-aloud to supplement the books in the bin; this will also give the whole club a book in common to have a conversation about.

If your selection of nonfiction books is very limited, then divide your reading time into two parts: informational reading for the first half of reading workshop, and fiction from book baggies for the second half of reading workshop. After each day's share, invite kids to spend ten or fifteen minutes reading their fiction book, and keep charts from your fiction or character units on display to support that work. Send those fiction books home, as well as the nonfiction books (or instead of them, if your supply of nonfiction is especially low). It is imperative that children have plenty to read and are not cycling through the same books over and over again, and certainly not resorting to books that are too hard.

Strategically design groups of four children to become book clubs.

Prior to launching the unit, you will want to start to think about how to assign students to nonfiction book clubs. Ideally, groups of four children who all read at approximately the same level would make for convenient groupings, so that they can easily swap books, and you can meet with those groups to introduce new books that all can read. On the other hand, you may decide to assign some children to mixed-level (heterogeneous) groupings. It will be very important that children are placed in clubs that they can work well in, sharing materials and managing daily conversations.

The readers in your class will come together not only because they read around the same level but also out of a shared curiosity about particular topics. Readers might circle the classroom with a clipboard, interview questions, and a list of possible topics, asking other students, "Do you want to learn more about wolves?" or "Which of the following topics sounds most interesting to you: whales, plants, or simple machines?" In this way, students take charge of finding like-minded peers with whom to form nonfiction book clubs. Then, of course, you'll take their suggestions and requests into account when you sit down to plan the groupings strategically, based on interests, reading habits, and reading levels.

The clubs will read from the same bin of books for an entire week, and then will choose a new topic bin. The books in the bin should be at the group's just-right level (there may need to be a mix of levels in the bin), or possibly a bit easier—but never containing books that are too hard for children to understand and read with fluency and accuracy.

Display relevant anchor charts from previous units of study.

This unit is unlikely to be the first nonfiction unit of study you've taught in the school year, so it makes sense then to gather up and revisit the anchor charts from previous units. In first grade, you might gather up your charts from *Learning About the World: Reading Nonfiction* (Unit 2), as well as your anchor charts from your information-writing units of study, particularly if you've taught *Nonfiction Chapter Books* (Unit 2).

Second-graders may have already had *Becoming Experts: Reading Nonfiction* (Unit 2), so you might refer to those charts as well as the charts from the writing unit, *Lab Reports and Science Books* (Unit 2).

Charts from writing that highlight text structures, or show examples of different ways information books might be organized, will be helpful to revisit in this unit.

You might also want to make further reading-writing connections by displaying any nonfiction mentor texts you've used in writing workshop. Perhaps you used *Sharks!* by Anne Schreiber as a mentor text for nonfiction chapter books, or *Forces and Motion (Hands-on Science)* by John Graham as a mentor text with second-graders. These books will be helpful to have on hand for this unit, as will any other informational books your students are highly familiar with.

Plan read-alouds and shared reading to support the work of this unit.

Consider that your read-aloud time can function as a maxi-version of a class book club, so during conversations you can mentor children in the kind of independent thinking and discussion moves you hope they will carry into their own book clubs.

During read-aloud and shared-reading time, you can arrange for students to sit near their book clubs, so that they only need to turn around to be able to talk in small circles of four or five students, rather than to a single partner as they have done in the past. Strategically seat the clubs so that those that need the most support from you are sitting close by, up front and center. During times when clubs are talking to one another, you'll want to be able to move about all the groups easily, so you might teach kids to leave a wide margin around the edge of your meeting area, as well as a path down the middle, so that you can easily move about, getting to the back of the meeting area easily and quickly.

Select books to read aloud that are of high interest but also lend themselves to the work of the unit. You may want also to match your read-aloud to some of the clubs' topic bins to give those clubs some extra background knowledge and practice with the topic. Ideally, you will want to read aloud several texts in a row on a topic, beginning with the easiest or most general of the books, to build a bit of vocabulary, and then move to the harder and more complex of the books.

As you move from read-aloud to read-aloud, you'll want to model some of the same work you'll be teaching in the unit. For example, you may want to model previewing the text to consider how each section is structured, and then involve the students in making a plan for how to read each section. When you encounter a how-to section for example, you'll want to dramatize each step, pretending to follow the steps to make sure they make sense. When you come to a timeline or a life-cycle section, you'll take care to retell the main events of the timeline in order to be sure you understand how one thing leads to another.

You'll also want to use read-aloud as an opportunity for children to practice jotting notes about the text and then using those notes to talk with their clubs. On chart paper or on a document camera you can model stopping to jot your own questions or ideas about the book, and then invite students to do the same. Kids can compare and add to their ideas, talking in groups, and then as a whole class. You can also collect Post-its kids have jotted and demonstrate how to organize information, sorting Post-its into categories, or putting them into chronological order, then inviting kids to add to the notes by talking with their clubs.

Teach them how to grow ideas from those notes, coaching by asking kids questions such as, "What does this make you think?" or "What ideas are you having now?"

In read-aloud and shared reading, you will want to read aloud books that lend themselves to comparing and contrasting. Finding two books on the same topic that are written in very different styles is a great place to begin. Perhaps one book is written from first-person perspective: "I am a giant panda. I live in the mountains of China," and the next is written in the passive voice, sounding much more academic.

In shared reading, you may want to choose one engaging, high-interest nonfiction text for each bend of the unit, using it to apply all the strategies kids know: self-monitoring, word solving, rereading, fluency, stopping and thinking, rereading some more, and so on. This unit is largely a comprehension unit, so you may want to use your shared reading to supplement with special attention to word-solving strategies and solving new and unfamiliar vocabulary.

BEND I: INDIVIDUALS BRING THEIR STRENGTHS AS NONFICTION READERS TO CLUBS

Launch the work of the unit by recruiting the kids to help reorganize the nonfiction books in your classroom library.

One of the best parts about reading nonfiction is the vast array of topics one might choose to read about. Once clubs are formed, you'll want to help your students see that the baskets of nonfiction in your classroom library are filled with books that they want to read. Too often, nonfiction books are presented as all work, and no enjoyment. You will want to launch this unit by making your classroom library as inviting and accessible as possible. Perhaps you'll place several baskets of mixed nonfiction books at each table, and invite the newly formed book clubs to sort the books into topics. You can provide a strategic mix of books at each table to help facilitate this, and sprinkle favorite nonfiction read-alouds into the mix as well. This work will help your students become familiar with what's available to choose from at their levels—and they can practice some strategies for previewing the text and making predictions about what each book might mostly be about.

Invite students to make labels for these baskets, and then gather in the meeting area so that each club can share the baskets of books they created. The topics, of course, will depend on what books you have available. The more books you have, the more specific the categories will probably be: "Polar Bears," "Pandas," "Snow Leopards." If you have fewer books, the categories will probably be broader: "Animals," "Plants," "Weather," "Transportation." You can encourage children to come up with clever names for the baskets they create: "Amazing Weather," "Incredible Plants," "Awesome Vehicles." If you are fortunate enough to have plenty of books, these baskets will also match the group's approximate independent reading levels (perhaps erring on the easy side if needed, in order to include more books on a topic). If you have fewer books, kids can read from topic baskets containing a wider mix of levels, and can learn a few strategies for navigating harder texts, although you do want to be sure that students are not spending the majority of their time reading books that are too hard for them.

As you enter this first week, you might also make a quick list of the skills and strategies your students already know, from past nonfiction units and even past years of school. You might revisit some of your old anchor charts, to use as visual reminders for what they have already learned about nonfiction reading, and you might plan a string of minilessons and mid-workshop teaching at the start of the unit to remind kids of the work they did in the last nonfiction unit, to get things up and running again.

You'll want to emphasize at this point that the most essential thing they can do as nonfiction readers is to monitor for meaning and to learn what each book is mostly about. They probably know how to preview the text to make predictions regarding what the book will mostly be about, to use their voices to read fluently and with intonation, and to determine the main topic or idea of a section, as well as the supporting details. By now, they also know to note the specific words an author uses and to use that language as they talk. If your students struggle with all these things, then you might consider switching to the "Growing Expertise in Little Books: Nonfiction Reading" unit of study (in this book) in place of this one.

> **"Readers, today I want to teach you that you need not start from scratch when you read a new book! You already know many strategies to use when reading nonfiction books. You can use the charts in our classroom as a reminder of all the reading work you already know how to do. Any time you pick up a book, before you even start reading, always think, 'What kind of text is this? What strategies do I know for reading this kind of text?'"**

If your classroom is short on nonfiction books, you may want to divide your workshop into two parts: a time for nonfiction reading from topic baskets and talking with book clubs, and the remainder of the time for reading from independent (leveled) book baggies, with a mix of nonfiction and other books. This way each student will have plenty of books to read. As students dive into their topic baskets, you'll want to circulate from table to table, giving compliments and reminders, and encouraging kids to read whole books, not just simply dip in and dip out to certain parts. You can interrupt the class from time to time, to give the whole class a reminder or a compliment, encouraging them to use everything they already know about nonfiction reading. As the time for reading about a topic comes to an end, you can teach kids to use a Post-it with their name on it to mark their place in the book they were reading before they return it to the basket.

Reinforce the strategies children already know and introduce new, more sophisticated ones, so that their growing repertoire matches the complexity of their new texts.

It is important that as you teach you reinforce the notion that children can draw on both old and new strategies, deciding which will work best for them in any one moment and book. For instance, "Nonfiction readers read with explaining voices" is a teaching point you may have taught in the past while working on fluency and intonation. Now you might remind students of this, but lift the level a bit as you do so. You might say, "Nonfiction readers don't just *read* with explaining voices; nonfiction readers also *talk* about the text with explaining voices! Readers can explain the text to themselves as they go along. They pause after reading for a bit, and use their own words if they can. This helps them understand the text better, and it prepares them to teach other club members about their topics." Even as you teach children to phrase and use intonation as they read, you can also prompt them to summarize the text in their own words, and prepare for talking with their club members.

Of course, you will also want students to use talking about the text as a tool for monitoring for sense. When it's difficult to explain the text to yourself or others, that means it's time to go back to reread more closely and carefully, really paying attention to the pictures and the words, making sure to really look at all the words, and to stop and think more often to be sure that everything is making sense. And when that isn't working, and it's happening across most of a book—it's time to pick a different book!

Teach students to preview their books for text structures, and then make a plan for how to best read each section of the book.

When students read nonfiction at earlier levels, each book was likely about a single topic, and often the whole book featured one text structure, for example: a book listing information on each page, or a how-to book with a new step or two on each page, or a pattern book. If a book was divided into subcategories of information, the subcategories were probably very clear. The books your students are reading now are more complex, possibly with a new text structure in each section (a life-cycle section, and a how-to section, and a section listing interesting facts, for example). Now, students will encounter different types of text structures and layouts, ones that may demand more flexibility with the kinds of strategies they use for determining the main idea. You may want to teach students how to preview the text with an eye toward text structure.

> **"Today I want to teach you that readers can get ready to read by taking a tour of all the pages in the book, from cover to cover, to see what kind of text structures the book contains. Then they can make a plan for how best to read each section."**

You can demonstrate starting a new book by reading the title, and noticing the cover, as usual. Next, highlight how you take a tour of all the pages of the book, from cover to cover, looking for clues about how the book is divided into sections, and how each section (as well as the entire book) is structured. It might be helpful to have a list of different text structures to be on the lookout for. How-to (or procedural) text, All About (or expository), Lists, Categories, Timelines or Life Cycles, Pros/Cons, Cause/Effect, Question/ Answer are all common text structures that your students might encounter—sometimes all of these appear in one book! Perhaps you'll model using a book where each section exemplifies a new text structure (Gail

Gibbons's books are perfect for this), and one book where the entire book is crafted in one text structure, such as question and answer. You might be able to make some connections to writing workshop here, and even refer to some familiar mentor texts from writing, if your students have written these types of texts. You may want to create a chart highlighting some of the most common text structures kids will come across (if you don't have one already):

Common Nonfiction Text Structures to Look Out For

- All-About (expository)
- How-To (procedural)
- Lists
- Categories
- Timelines or Life Cycles
- Pros/Cons
- Cause and Effect
- Question/Answer

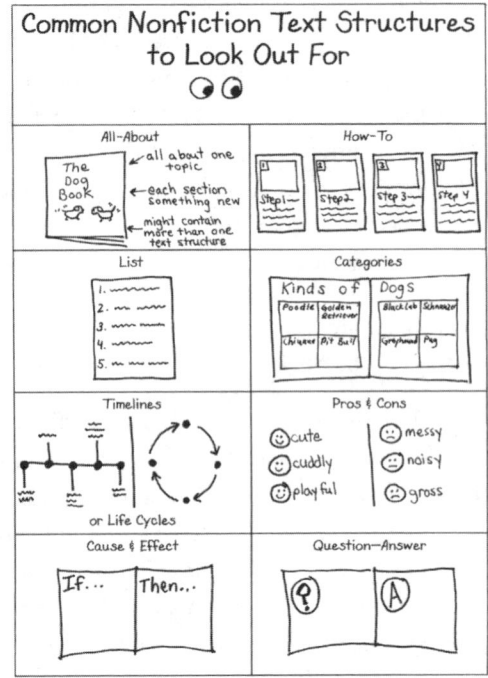

Of course, each text structure will call on the reader to do different kinds of work. A how-to section is best read with readers envisioning each step, imagining themselves following the directions to make sure that it makes sense. An expository text is often read in chunks, with the reader figuring out the main idea and key details of each chunk of text, then putting it all together to figure out what the whole thing was mostly about. A question-and-answer text calls on readers to read the question and then think, "Hmm, . . . What could the answer be?" and predict before they read the answer section—then check and revise their prediction as they read. You may want to do a string of mid-workshop teaching, combined with some conferring and small-group work where you briefly model a few ways to read each text structure, and of course highlight that the table of contents (if the book has one) is often a giant clue for how the whole book will be structured.

At the end of that day's workshop, you might ask students to share all the different text structures they were able to find, along with naming a few strategies they used for reading that type of text structure. Or perhaps you'll share a few examples of text structures that have appeared in familiar read-alouds. You may decide to add to your text structures chart, using photocopies of key pages from familiar books, or adding a note about different strategies readers use to tackle each structure. You might decide to do a follow-up mini-lesson or two to highlight how to read specific text structures that your students seem to have trouble with.

Teach students how to navigate more complex texts, accumulating the most important information as they read.

In denser texts, the work of accumulating information across the pages becomes all the more essential to comprehension. One of the big challenges for students reading transitional levels is that the books they are now reading are much longer than what they had become accustomed to in earlier levels—and each level just keeps getting longer and more packed full of surprising details, interesting facts, and more and more information to sort through. Often at these levels, authors will explain something early on that becomes a key to understanding a later part of the text—if students miss that information in the beginning of the book, it can throw off their understanding of the parts that come later. Because of the sheer amount of information, kids will need to learn how to figure out which information is important enough to remember and hang on to, and which information is helpful but not crucial.

When this unit began, you may have noticed that many children have a tendency to remember interesting, but not necessarily important facts. Some teachers call these "wow facts," as in, "Wow! What a cool fact!" or "Wow! That's so weird/gross/disgusting/amazing! I can't wait to tell people about it." Being a "wow" fact collector is not always such a bad thing. After all, these readers are engaged and interested in their books. Often, adults compliment and even encourage kids to retain this kind of information. In fact, your students need not look far to find messages supporting the idea that remembering trivia is one thing that will make people think you are very smart. Quiz shows and trivia games abound.

We don't want to teach kids completely out of the habit of fact-collecting, but we do want them to be able to think more deeply about the information they read. And more than that, we become especially concerned when the attempt to retain trivial information gets in the way of being able to comprehend the whole of the text—as often is the case when students begin to read longer and more complex books. Often, there simply isn't enough mental energy to store all that trivia *and* figure out the main ideas, much less come up with more sophisticated thoughts about the text.

So for the next part of this bend, you will probably want to teach a number of strategies that help children accumulate the text across these longer books they are now reading, and to determine what is important.

One first step is to be sure students know how to break the longer text apart into manageable sections. Teach children to preview the text looking for clues about where the sections might be, and that they will need to stop and think often as they read each section, thinking, "Hmm, . . . Does all this information fit together? How does it fit together? What's it *mostly* about?" Of course, nonfiction books provide lots of clues for figuring this out. Headings and subheadings are big clues—these are somewhat obvious markers for sections. But also, each new page often marks off a new section (especially in nonchapter books), as do paragraphs (in nearly all books). Pictures can also help with breaking the text into meaningful sections—when you see a picture in a nonfiction book, it likely is related to what one of the sections is mostly about—although readers do have to watch out for "Wow!" pictures, just as they need to watch out for "wow facts." With each section of the text, readers must stop and think, "What is this *mostly* about?"

Of course, figuring out what each section is mostly about isn't always so easy, so you may need to teach a few ways readers do this work. One strategy is to look for words and phrases that repeat. After all, if it was important enough for the author to repeat, then it probably relates to a main idea. Another strategy is to encourage kids to read for key details using the "5W's (and H)": Who? What? When? Where? Why? How? That is, readers stop and think often, "Who or what is this mostly about? When or where is this taking place? Why is this happening or why is it important? How does this work?" Your students will benefit if this is woven into your read-alouds across time, so that they can see how to use these questions flexibly across many books, because every book is different. The question, "When or where is this taking place?" works differently, for example, in a book about penguins, where the book is clearly set in Antarctica, than in a book about trucks, for example, that doesn't name a setting. These questions are helpful as long as students are able to figure out which questions apply, and which do not, and aren't using them in a rigidly literal fashion. When these questions are new, it may help students to have a mini-chart to refer to, or a bookmark as a reminder:

Readers Hang On to Key Details

- Who or what is this mostly about?
- What is happening?
- When or where is this taking place?
- Why is this happening? Why is this important?
- How does this work?

When you teach children to break a longer text into meaningful sections, you are helping them to be able to figure out main ideas and key details of smaller, separate chunks. Then, you may need to teach them how to put it all back together again. You won't want children to fall into the habit of reading each new section as if it were totally unrelated to the section before (and this is a common habit). Teach children that it helps to synthesize information across an entire text, thinking, "How does this section fit with the one before it?" or "What are both of these pages talking about?" When you teach kids to synthesize, you are teaching them how to fit together the separate parts of the text. They may need support synthesizing the information just on a page that has multiple parts to it. Or perhaps some kids will need more support with synthesizing information across several pages—putting together the pieces of information from across a chapter or longer section. Certainly many children will need support with synthesizing the information across the entire book, asking themselves, "How do all these pieces connect? How do they go together?"

> "Today I want to teach you that readers don't just read each page or section of their book separately. They gather information across an entire book, thinking, 'How does this page fit with the one before it?' Other times, they'll want to pause, section by section, thinking, 'How does this part fit with the one before it?' or 'What are both of these parts talking about?'"

Key Details
Mini-Charts or Bookmarks

Readers Hang On to Key Details	Readers Hang On to Key Details	Readers Hang On to Key Details	Readers Hang On to Key Details
WHO or WHAT is this mostly about?	WHO or WHAT is this mostly about?	WHO or WHAT is this mostly about?	WHO or WHAT is this mostly about?
WHAT is happening?	WHAT is happening?	WHAT is happening?	WHAT is happening?
WHEN or WHERE is this taking place?	WHEN or WHERE is this taking place?	WHEN or WHERE is this taking place?	WHEN or WHERE is this taking place?
WHY is this happening? WHY is this important?	WHY is this happening? WHY is this important?	WHY is this happening? WHY is this important?	WHY is this happening? WHY is this important?
HOW does this work?	HOW does this work?	HOW does this work?	HOW does this work?

Teach students a few strategies for preparing for great conversations with their book clubs.

As kids read, you'll want to encourage them to use all that you've taught so far in this unit: using text structure to preview the text, figuring out the important information as they read, as well as synthesizing it—figuring out how everything connects. But you'll also want them to be thinking about what to talk about with their club members. The best conversations happen when kids come ready to talk. Since they will all be reading different titles, you might begin by teaching them some simple but engaging ways that they can summarize what they've read.

You might say, "As you are reading, one thing you can do is to dramatize what you see in the pictures, or what you are picturing in your mind." Teach kids to envision the animals, plants, machines—or whatever they are reading about. "Don't just picture it like a photograph in your mind—make that picture move. Bring it to life. What does it really look like when it moves? What does it sounds like? Move your own body to try it out. This will help you understand your book better; then when you are teaching your club members what you learned in your book, you can pick parts to *show* them what you've learned—and they can try it, too!"

Teaching this as one of the very first things clubs learn to do together will help guarantee that club time is engaging and interesting for kids (and reinforces their understanding of the books). As you listen in on clubs talking and dramatizing parts, you might find that their conversations seem disconnected. One kids dramatizes a part, then the next kid, then the next kid. There will be time for lifting the level of their conversations as the unit progresses. For now, encourage kids to ham it up and to let those dramatizations lead naturally into authentic conversations (and laughter) among the children. You might coach lightly, giving brief prompts such as, "Say more!" or "Do another one!" or "What do others think about that part?" or "Say a little bit about why you picked that part."

Each time clubmates meet, they will come prepared to share whatever information they learned on their own. The challenge will be to get students to do this in a way that reinforces discussion of main ideas, rather than recalling trivial facts. You might teach your students that each club member can use their hand and fingers as a way to organize and talk about what they've learned.

> **"Today I want to teach you that readers teach their clubmates the main ideas of what they've learned. You can use your hand and your five fingers to help you stay organized. Point to your palm and say the main idea, then point to each finger to give an example to fit with the main idea."**

For example, a child might say, "The big thing I learned in *Role, Slope and Slide: A Book About Ramps* (by Michael Dahl) is what a ramp is. Then I learned how ramps help people and animals in the world." Then the child can touch each finger for each supporting piece of information. She might touch her pointer finger and say, "For example, ramps can help people in wheelchairs get into buildings with stairs," then touch her middle finger and say, "Another example of the way ramps help is . . ." and so on. By doing this, children are demonstrating their ability to identify the main purpose of the text, including what the author wants to answer, explain, or describe.

Remind children to draw on the support of their clubs when meaning breaks down.

Of course, sometimes children will struggle to teach information to their clubmates because they themselves haven't understood it. A big part of monitoring for meaning is knowing when you don't understand something and then drawing on tools to gain that understanding. When children have difficulty teaching what they read, they can bring their confusions or misunderstandings to their club and draw on the support of other members to clarify these. A child might say, "In my book it says that gravity holds us on the ground, but I don't really get it. Did your book talk about that?" or "I thought that astronauts walk in space, but in the book it says that they are in free fall because there is no gravity in space. I don't get it."

Before the clubs move on to the next bend in the unit (choosing new topic baskets to read from) you will want to encourage them to determine what is important about their topic, or what areas they might want to study and think about more closely. You might remind them that, "Information book clubs decide what parts about a topic they want to study more closely. Can you all, as a club, come up with three to five different things you want to study about your topic? Think about what you are hoping to get out of this work. You decide." This will provide clubs with jumping-off points as they grow ideas and compare and contrast across texts for the last day or so of this bend.

BEND II: NONFICTION CLUBS ADD THEIR OWN IDEAS TO WHAT THEY LEARN

Introduce the work of this bend.

The focus of this bend in the unit is adding one's own thinking about reading. It's important, however, for you to emphasize that children *add* their own thoughts, ideas, and opinions to the information—not *replace* the information with their own made-up material. We don't mean to suggest that students should read something about trees and then add, "I think trees can be magical and drop fruit that glows in the dark!" Instead, we expect students to begin to ask and answer questions and make speculations that are accountable to the text. That is, they use the information to grow an idea, and then provide text support for that idea.

You might begin this bend by saying something like, "Since the beginning of this month, each of you has demonstrated just how careful you are as nonfiction readers. You've learned to use text structure to make a plan for how to read your books, you've learned to break your books up into manageable sections, and to put all the separate pieces of information together and think about the main topics or ideas. You've learned to read from cover to cover, making a picture in your mind, and how to teach your clubmates what you've been learning. Now you'll continue to do all of that *plus* you'll be working hard to grow big ideas about your books. One of the best things about being in a book club is getting to hear everyone's different ideas about the topic. As you are reading, you are not only learning information—but that information can lead you to new ideas."

> **"Today I want to teach you that expert nonfiction readers do more than just learn information from their books, they also come up with their own ideas about what they are learning. Readers sometimes push themselves to have an idea by thinking, 'The idea I'm having is . . .' or 'I think . . .' Readers come up with a great idea, jot it on a Post-it, and then read on, looking for parts of the book that fit with their idea."**

You might make connections to other units where you have taught students to grow ideas—perhaps in a fiction unit of study, or series books, or in fairy tales. Certainly during read-aloud time you will have been practicing coming up with ideas and then supporting them with evidence from the text. Perhaps even in writing workshop your students may have been learning about how to develop opinions. Remind children that the work they are doing in their nonfiction reading is not all that different from work they have done elsewhere.

Here is one of those times when the materials do make a difference. You may be tempted to wonder—do they have to use Post-its? Can't they just practice thinking and talking about their ideas? In this case, the Post-its are going to play an important role. Not only will these make your students' thinking visible (for you and for themselves), but the ideas they jot will become invaluable tools for lifting the level of their book club conversation. There is also the bonus that for some kids, the Post-its themselves are an enticement to stop and think.

Teach children strategies to push their thinking about nonfiction books.

One way readers infer and grow ideas is by reacting to the information in the books they read. Once they understand what the author is saying, they mull over their reaction to it—eventually landing on an inference. Kids might think, "Wow, it's amazing that gravity is so strong that it pulls everything down! It must take a lot of force for a jet to fly so far off the ground. I wonder what makes that kind of force." Notice the inference comes after the reaction. You'll want to teach your children to push past "Wow!" to explain their thinking using details from the text. Teach them to use that initial reaction to think further and grow a full-fledged idea.

Once you have this work going, you will want to study children's Post-its as an informal form of data. There are some typical patterns in their responses that you might notice. Some kids will jot down facts, or very literal summaries, and call them "ideas." These are kids that need extra support with generating complete ideas, thoughts, and opinions based on the text, and not simply reactions such as "Wow!" or "Cool!" You might gather them as a group and teach them a few prompts (sometimes called "talk stems"). "This makes me think . . ." or "In my opinion . . ." or "I agree/disagree with the part where . . ." Of course, if the majority of your students fit this description, then this may be your next minilesson.

Other students may have no trouble generating ideas—but those ideas appear to be only loosely related to what they are reading. Sometimes children (and readers of all ages) will have a tendency to rely too heavily on their prior knowledge, and are not paying close enough attention to what the book is actually about. For example, a child who has grown up on a farm and is reading about cows writes, "Milking is hard work." Meanwhile the book hasn't mentioned milking at all—it is actually about different types of cows. Or a student who knows a lot about sharks says, "Sharks are actually very playful," but the book she happens to be holding contains information to the contrary—that sharks conserve their energy and are fierce predators.

It isn't that these children are wrong—it's that they aren't reading their books closely. You might teach some strategies for being more accountable to the text and for reading more closely. For example, you might say to students, "Today I want to teach you that readers don't just think, 'What do I already personally know about this topic?' Instead they think, 'What is this book actually about?'" You might role-play in a very obvious way being the kind of reader who has his or her own ideas about a topic, regardless of what the text actually says, then pause to ask the students what you should do differently. "Reread! Read it again!" they might say. Or they might, wisely, say, "What part of the book goes with that? Find it! Prove it!" Of course, if students do not come up with this advice for you, you can always say, "I suppose I ought to reread, right? And it seems I should probably find a place in the book that actually proves what I am saying? And if I cannot? Maybe I should see if I can come up with an idea that *is* based on what I've read."

Another way to generate ideas about a book is to consider the "author's intent" or the "author's purpose" in writing the book. Of course, as readers, all we can do is generate theories, unless we happen to have access to the actual author to find out for sure. This work helps children generate ideas, while staying within the "four walls" of the text. You might teach children that authors often write for several reasons: to persuade, to inform, or to entertain are three classic examples. Of course, writers write for reasons beyond those three basics as well. And of course, sometimes writers write for a whole combination of reasons—we can enjoy coming up with educated guesses, and we can use our guesses as an entry point to reading the text more closely.

For example, the book *Bugs! Bugs! Bugs!* by Jennifer Dussling could be interpreted in multiple ways. One child may confidently claim that the author's purpose was clearly to inform, and that is why she included so many specific facts, and why she wrote the book in such a clearly organized way. Another child might state that no, the author actually wanted to entertain us—that's why she used such funny comparisons, and that's why she picked out such creepy and sometimes disgusting examples (like the beetle that turns your skin into soup—disgusting!). A third child might make a justifiable claim that no, actually, *Bugs! Bugs! Bugs!* is meant to persuade us not to be so afraid of bugs. The author clearly states, "Yikes! Bugs look scary close up. But *you* don't need to worry. Most bugs are a danger only to other insects. They are the bugs that really bug other bugs."

These are high-level conversations for youngsters to be having. Model thinking about author's purpose during read-aloud so that over time students hear many examples of how to support an idea with examples and information from the text. Be sure to model rereading with an idea in mind during read-alouds. Then, during independent reading and club time, encourage kids to develop their own theories and go looking for examples and evidence to support their ideas. Coach students to reread often, to use pictures as well as the words to find support for their ideas, and to ask their club members questions to help each other support their ideas.

Teach children to revise their thinking as they read and see more in a text.

You also want to teach your students to be flexible thinkers. They enter a book confident of what they know about a topic. As they read on, rather than holding firm to their preconceived beliefs, encourage them to be open to learning more and revising their thinking if needed.

> "Today I want to teach you that readers are flexible with their thinking. They read with an open mind, thinking, 'Yes. This confirms what I knew.' They *also* think, 'Oh! This is different than what I thought I knew.' During club meetings, readers can talk about how their thinking has changed."

In some cases, this means confirming what they know and adding to their knowledge any related information from the book. In other instances, it means taking what they *thought* they knew and explaining why they had the misconceptions they did. This, of course, will often lead them to grow new ideas. During club meetings, they might use sentence starters like those that follow to share their new understanding and ideas:

- I used to think . . . but now I'm thinking . . .
- My new thinking was about . . . but it's now different because . . .
- I thought I knew something about . . . but then I read this part that says . . . so now I think . . .
- I was right about . . . and I also learned . . . so now I think . . .

As your readers learn to ask questions of their text, you might teach them some questions that almost always lead to deeper thinking, such as: "How do . . . ?," "Why do . . . ?," "How come . . . ?," and "Why would . . . ?" Pursuing a question in a single book and, especially, in several related books, can drive a child or club's reading. Imagine a club reading through all its force and motion books, looking for the answer to this question: "Since there is no air in space and no air friction, what would happen if I threw a ball in space?" Even if the club members don't find the answer, they can use the information they *do* find to suggest a possible answer. This requires that they're able to synthesize related information to form ideas. They might then say, "Well, since it says here . . . I'll bet . . ."

Teach children strategies for embedding their thinking into the text.

You might also teach readers to embed their thinking about the text by making their own picture caption or adding to an existing caption, writing it on a Post-it or removable tape. Perhaps a reader first discovers that centrifugal force will cause objects to be pushed back if there is a great amount of acceleration. She might add a caption that states that centrifugal force is what she has experienced on some amusement park rides.

Teach students to have conversations about the topic as a whole.

As you near the end of this bend, remember that your students have been reading books on the same topic as the other members of their book club. You may want to teach some strategies for helping students have conversations about the topic as a whole, going beyond talking about one book at time. This will require that they make connections across all the books they've been reading—made all the more challenging if they've read different titles from one another. You might support their work by providing large chart paper for students to map out their thinking about the topic as a whole. In a minilesson, you might show students two or three different ways to organize the main ideas they have been learning. "Today I want to teach you that readers often choose a way to organize the information they learned from what they've read," you might say. "As you work with your club, talk to each other about the topic you've been studying. What are the main ideas you've learned? You can use writing to organize your ideas and supporting information."

Ideally you would have already used a few different tools for organizing information during read-aloud and shared reading, so that kids are already familiar with several options. Then you might quickly review them all in one minilesson. Otherwise, you might select the one that seems the most appropriate for the bulk of your class, and then teach the others to small groups. A semantic web makes a lot of sense, visually, for many kids. A web lends itself to basic sorting and categorizing—perfect for combining facts coming from separate books. A T-chart might be introduced as a way to organize pros and cons of one aspect of the topic, or causes and effects, or information on one side, and ideas on the other. A T-chart can show the relationship between two kinds of information. And a third option might be for students, as a group, to create a large labeled diagram or picture that represents the most important aspects of what they've learned. This open-ended diagram option might be particularly suited to students reading easier books or students who are not fluent writers. As students work together on any of these representations of what they've learned about their topic, there will be many opportunities for them to practice going back to the books for text evidence, and to reread to get new ideas for what to say and add to the group's knowledge.

As students work together, combining their information and discussing the topic, you will want to encourage them to talk together about why the topic they've been studying is important. For instance, a club that has been learning about forces and motion might together decide that if gravity can be used for water wheels to create electricity, perhaps there are more ways that natural resources can be used. This club might then decide to make some posters at home to let others know that we can help our environment by learning about other natural resources that can create electricity, which helps global warming.

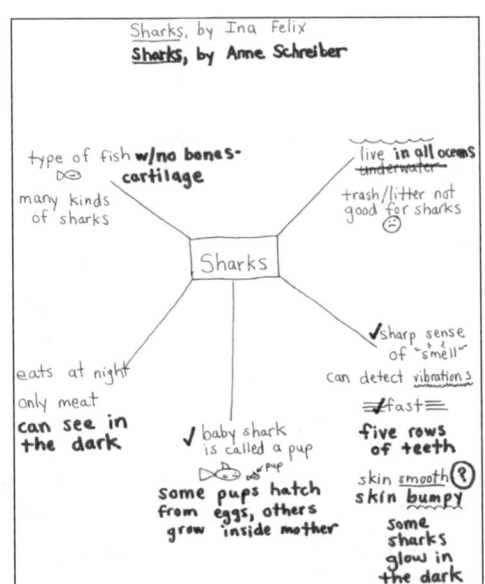

Using a semantic web provides a visual support for understanding how the information from separate sources fits together. During read-aloud, this teacher used two different pens to help students keep track of which text the information came from.

Children can thus express their ideas about the importance of what they are learning as ethical concerns and/or as action plans.

> **"Readers don't just absorb information—they think about why what they are learning is so important. When something they read seems very important they can take action: they can teach others why their topic is so important."**

To wrap up this bend, you might end with a mini-celebration where clubs put their charts and posters on display for others to learn about their topic—and perhaps to help the other clubs decide what topic they would like to read about next. These charts aren't meant to be "final projects" at all, rather, more like the group's notes about the topic, made large and shareable. As students move about the room to visit each club's work, they might leave Post-its on the charts with questions or comments about the information, for the club to look over together and discuss.

BEND III: NONFICTION CLUBS COMPARE AND CONTRAST INFORMATION ABOUT TOPICS

Set children up to compare and contrast information about a topic.

Hopefully, if your students are reading at the levels this unit is aimed toward, they have already done some comparing and contrasting on their own, without much prompting, in the last two bends. Perhaps, for example, two different readers shared information from two different books about force and motion: "My book says . . ." or "That's weird, because my book says . . ." Or perhaps they compared information within the same book: "On this page it talks about . . . but here, it says . . ." In this bend, you'll teach kids how to compare and contrast the information in their books in meaningful ways—ways that lead to deeper thinking about each book, and about the topic in general.

To launch this bend, you might share an example of a book, or create a piece of your own writing, that leaves out key pieces of information. Then share a book that fills in those missing pieces to give a whole new meaning to the topic. Take the example of sharks as a topic. There are many books that highlight sharks being vicious predators. You might read aloud a particularly vivid chapter about sharks as predators, for example, the introduction from *Sharks* by Anne Schreiber (published by National Geographic Kids).

CHOMP!
What is quick?
What is quiet?
What has five rows of teeth?
What glides through the water?

Sharks, by Anne Schreiber	
We learned...	This makes us think...
sharks have cartilage instead of bones to move + bend easily	Maybe it helps them hunt/fight/escape for survival?
some pups hatch from eggs, others grow inside mother shark	Sharks are VERY different from other fish. what else is different?
sharks can smell a drop of blood from miles away	The must travel far to catch their prey
sharks go through 10,000 teeth in their lifetime	The teeth must grow fast- sharks need them to survive. W/o sharp teeth they can't hunt.
some sharks have camoflage to blend w/ ocean floor	If they have to move habitats they won't blend in anymore.

During read-aloud, this teacher used a T-chart to help students hang on to information *and* grow ideas.

CHOMP!

It's a shark!

Then immediately read aloud a section from a book describing sharks as an endangered species, who are often misunderstood and are carelessly overfished, victims of bycatch and finning, often treated in inhumane ways. For example, the book *Sharks* by Ina Felix presents sharks as friendly and misunderstood. She writes from the first-person point of view, causing the reader to empathize with the shark rather than view it as threat. For example, she writes:

I have many sharp teeth. We are often feared because of our appearance but we are really wonderful animals!

Sharks come in many different shapes and sizes. The whale shark in considered to be the biggest type of shark.

My mom and dad are gentle giants.

I have a lovely wide grin.

I have an awesome sense of smell.

Setting two distinctly different sources of information side by side this way you can help students understand that while the first book wasn't incorrect, exactly, there was much more to learn about the topic by reading more books, and comparing the information from the two books to come up with one big idea: sharks are misunderstood creatures.

> "Today I want to teach you that most nonfiction books only contains bits and pieces of the whole truth about a topic. Every author has to pick and choose what to include and what to leave out—there simply isn't room in one book to include everything! So one thing that readers do is think, 'What's missing from this book?' and 'How is this book the same or different from other books on this topic?'"

You can also show children how they can lay two (or three, or even four) books side by side to notice and name what is similar and what is different about their books. In the past, when your students were reading easier books, they may have had a tendency to name trivial similarities and differences. "My book has a bird in it!" one kid may have exclaimed. "Mine, too!" another may have said upon comparing the two books. "My bird has a beak!" "Me, too!" When students do this, you can encourage them to stretch this further, saying why those details matter. "Why is this important?" they might ask each other, or "Why do you think this keeps showing up in all the books?"

While this may be a first step toward comparing and contrasting, there will of course be times when those tiny details are just that—tiny. Clinging to extraneous information won't help students hang on to what their books are mostly about or generate meaningful ideas, thoughts, and opinions about their books. You might teach students that when they lay their books side by side, of course they might notice the tiny details that are the same or different—but they can *also* name what each chapter or section was *mostly* about to compare it to other books (and sections within other books). They can then begin to notice which books have similar main ideas, and which books contain new main ideas.

Teach your readers that when they notice differences it's helpful to *first* consider what makes two things different, and *then* to think about what might explain the differences. For example, the observation "If you push a toy car along a shiny wooden hallway, it rolls much farther than if you push it along a thick bedroom rug" (the difference exists in the surface) might lead to the explanation that there is more friction in a thick rug than there is on a wooden floor, and friction slows things down. As your clubs compare and contrast the information in their books, be sure to support them as they incorporate more nuanced language to describe the information they are comparing and contrasting. For example, a chart might look this:

Readers Compare and Contrast Books

- In this section . . . but in this section . . .
- In this book . . . but in this book . . .
- The difference between . . . and . . . is . . .
- What's the same about these two . . . is . . .
- Unlike the . . . in this book the . . . does [doesn't] . . .
- When we were learning about . . . we learned . . . but now that we're learning . . .

As the unit continues, clubs might begin to create categories of information, and collect important examples, facts, details, and quotes under each category from across their books. Teach them to look across their Post-its as a group to figure out ways to organize the information they've collected, noting where club members have collected similar information, and where they've found differences.

> "Today I want to teach you that when readers are trying to make sense of a text, it helps to look across their Post-its and ideas, either on the same page or across pages. First, they figure out a way to organize all of their information. And then they look at their Post-its, side by side, and ask, 'How are these the same and how are they different?'"

Clubs might use the categories or big ideas they have been building across their study to help them put information together in meaningful ways. Have them place their Post-its, from a similar category, side by side. Then channel them to ask themselves (and their clubmates), "How are these the same and how are these different?"

As children find parts in their books that fit together, teach them how to talk about and compare the parts that are similar. Inevitably, as children find and note similarities, they'll discover differences, too, or at least will engage in a conversation about differences. Help kids lay out their texts and Post-its side by side so they can move easily between the texts and Post-its, citing examples and thoughts. Sometimes when children work together, they forget to go back and read from the text to give an example. Teach students to prompt one another by asking, "Where does it say that? Is there another example? Prove it!"

As the bend continues, each club member will have read a number of books on the topic, and will have likely encountered nonfiction books written in different styles. Sometimes the books they encounter are written in a more artistic style. Sometimes the author decides to write in first person ("I am an apple tree. These are my leaves."); other times an author writes in a zany, almost comical style (as in the National Geographic Readers transportation series, which contains speech bubbles, jokes in the sidebars, and silly characters). Now is the perfect time to teach children that they can also compare and contrast the styles of different books.

> "Today I want to teach you that readers can also read like writers, comparing and contrasting the styles of different books. They notice an author's choices and think, 'How is the style of this book similar to the style of another book? How is it different? Why did the author write it this way?'"

In a minilesson, you might select two very different informational books on the same topic to compare the authors' choice of words, sentence length, tone, mood, and other stylistic choices. *Sky Tree* by Thomas Locker and Candace Christiansen, for example, is written almost in poetry, with attention to tiny details, lots of figurative language, and illustrated with oil paintings, rather than photographs or diagrams, that convey the same tree changing across the seasons.

Once a tree
stood alone on a hill by
the river. Through the
long days, its leaves
fluttered in the soft
summer breeze.

A *Tree for All Seasons*, on the other hand, is a National Geographic book by Robin Bernard. It is illustrated with vibrant photographs of close-in details of trees. The text contains more technical language, making it sound more like a "teaching book" than poetry—but it is still engaging and interesting. Both books are interesting and fun to read, both books show what happens to trees across four seasons, and both books contain overlapping facts and information. By pairing two books like this, you'll help kids do the same with their books—even if they don't find two examples quite as clearly different-yet-the-same as these.

As the bend comes to a close, you might invite clubs to go back to other topic baskets to practice some of the compare-and-contrast work from this bend that they didn't yet practice on those books. They might look for patterns—do some topics tend to be written about in a certain style more than others? Are there more poetic books about seasons, for example, than about forces and motion? Are there more funny books about animals than about recycling? It will be up to your students to investigate and then theorize on why that might be.

CELEBRATION

By now, your children are filled to the brim with information, ideas, and theories. They've learned volumes about different topics that excited them from the start, and chances are they're even more excited now. Instead of letting all of that knowledge go underground, think about ways they might spread their thrill of learning about a particular topic to other kids in the class. How might you get children who shied away from certain baskets earlier in the year eagerly anticipating reading what's in them now? One way is to have the students from the club that studied these topics introduce their books and teach their topic to the rest of their classmates.

Of course, there are other options for how to spread children's new information. Club members can mark pages that answer the questions they pursued as the unit unfolded, and present their findings to another club or to other teachers or guests. The presentation might feature a chart or a diagram. You might have a "museum" share in which visitors come to each book club to hear what children have learned. During these shares, clubs will assume the role of instructors, teaching the information from the texts they have read. However you decide to set children up to share the expert knowledge they grew as a club, make sure that they have a chance to reflect on how and why others might need to know this information, so that children understand that their learning has real-world consequences.

BEND I: INDIVIDUALS BRING THEIR STRENGTHS AS NONFICTION READERS TO CLUBS

- "Readers, today I want to teach you that you and your club members can sort the books from our classroom library into topics you might want to read about. You can use everything you know about previewing and predicting to make a guess about what each book is mostly about. For each book, you can say, 'Are there other books like this one? Are there other books that fit with this one? Are there other books on the same topic?' Books that go together can be put in the same basket."

- "Readers, today I want to teach you that you need not start from scratch when you read a new book! You already know many strategies to use when reading nonfiction books. You can use the charts in our classroom as a reminder of all the reading work you already know how to do. Any time you pick up a book, before you even start reading, always think, 'What kind of text is this? What strategies do I know for reading this kind of text?'"

- "Readers, today I want to teach you that nonfiction readers don't just *read* with explaining voices; nonfiction readers also *talk* about the text with explaining voices. Readers can practice explaining the text to themselves as they go along, using their own words. Then you can explain the text to your club members when it's time to talk."

- "Today I want to teach you that no matter what kind of book you are reading, you should always be able to make sense of the text. If you are having trouble explaining the text to yourself or to your partner in your own words, that's a sign that it's time to go back to the last place where things were making sense and reread, paying closer attention to what the book is mostly about."

- "Today I want to teach you that readers can get ready to read by taking a tour of all the pages in the book, from cover to cover, to see what kind of text structures the book contains. Then they can make a plan for how best to read each section."

- "Today I want to teach you that readers can break longer text apart into manageable sections. As they read they use clues to figure out how break the text the apart:
  - headings and subheadings
  - new pages
  - paragraphs
  - pictures"

Use this list as a menu of possibilities, selecting only the teaching points that meet the needs of your students. Use your assessment data (running records, conferring and small-group notes, observations, responses to read-alouds, and other information) to decide on a plan that is tailored to the needs of your class. These teaching points may be used as whole-class minilessons, mid-workshop teaching, or for conferences and small-group work. You need not use every teaching point. See the unit overview for guidelines on how much time to spend in each bend.

- With each section of the text, readers stop and think, 'What is this *mostly* about?'"

- "Readers stop and think often to hang on to key details in the text. They ask themselves:

  - Who or what is this mostly about?

  - What is happening?

  - When or where is this taking place?

  - Why is this happening? Why is this important?

  - How does this work?"

- "Today I want to teach you that readers don't just read each page or section of their book separately. They gather information across an entire book, thinking, 'How does this page fit with the one before it?' Other times, they'll want to pause, section by section, thinking, 'How does this part fit with the one before it?' or 'What are both of these parts talking about?'"

- "Today I want to teach you that it's important to come to your club time ready to talk. One of the ways you can share your book with your clubmates is by dramatizing what you see in the pictures or what you imagine in your head as you are reading."

- "Today I want to teach you that readers teach their clubmates the main ideas of what they've learned. You can use your hand and your five fingers to help you stay organized. Point to your palm and say the main idea, then point to each finger to give an example to fit with the main idea."

- "Today I want to remind you that clubmates can be a terrific source of support! When you struggle to understand something in your reading, don't be afraid to ask for help. Say, 'In my book, I read . . . and I don't understand this.' Or 'I read . . . in my book. Did any of you see something similar in your book? I thought . . . but . . .'"

BEND II: NONFICTION CLUBS ADD THEIR OWN IDEAS TO WHAT THEY LEARN

- "Today I want to teach you that expert nonfiction readers do more than just learn information from their books, they also come up with their own ideas about what they are learning. Readers sometimes push themselves to have an idea by thinking, 'The idea I'm having is . . .' or 'I think . . .' Readers come up with a great idea, jot it on a Post-it, and then read on, looking for parts of the book that fit with their idea."

- "Today I want to teach you that nonfiction readers push past 'wow' in their book. They respond to the information they learn in books. When something catches their attention, and they have an idea, they explain their thinking by using details from the text."

- "Today I want to teach you that readers don't just think, 'What do I personally already know about this topic?' Instead they think, 'What is this book actually about?'"

- Today I want to teach you that readers can consider the author's purpose in writing the book. We can come up with a theory based on what we know about the book. Authors often write to persuade, to inform, or to entertain."

- "Today I want to teach you that readers are flexible with their thinking. They read with an open mind, thinking, 'Yes. This confirms what I knew.' They *also* think, 'Oh! This is different than what I thought I knew.' During club meetings, readers can talk about how their thinking has changed."

- "Today I want to teach you that readers embed, or put their own thinking about the text right into the text, by making their own picture captions or adding to existing captions, writing theirs on a Post-it or removable tape."

- "Today I want to teach you that readers often choose a way to organize their information that matches what they've read. They look across all the information they have collected as a group and ask themselves, 'What are the main ideas we've learned? What are the categories? What's the best way to organize all this?' You can use writing to organize your ideas and supporting information."

- "Readers don't just absorb information—they think about why what they are learning is so important. When something they read seems very important they can take action: they can teach others why their topic is so important."

BEND III: NONFICTION CLUBS COMPARE AND CONTRAST INFORMATION ABOUT TOPICS

- "Today I want to teach you that most nonfiction books only contains bits and pieces of the whole truth about a topic. Every author has to pick and choose what to include and what to leave out—there simply isn't room in one book to include everything! So one thing that readers do is think, 'What's missing from this book?' and 'How is this book the same or different from other books on this topic?'"

- "Today I want to teach you that when readers lay their books side by side, they can name what each chapter or section was *mostly* about to compare it to other books (and sections within other books). They can then begin to notice which books have similar main ideas, and which books contain new main ideas."

- "Today I want to teach you that when readers are trying to make sense of a text, it helps to look across their Post-its and ideas, either on the same page or across pages. First, they figure out a way to organize all of their information. And then they look at their Post-its, side by side, and ask, 'How are these the same and how are they different?'"

- "Today I want to teach you that partners can hold each other accountable to the information in the actual text and using evidence from the text by prompting one another with questions like, 'Where does it say that? Is there another example? Prove it!'"

- "Today I want to teach you that readers can also read like writers, comparing and contrasting the styles of different books. They notice an author's choices and think, 'How is the style of this book similar to the style of another book? How is it different? Why did the author write it this way?'"

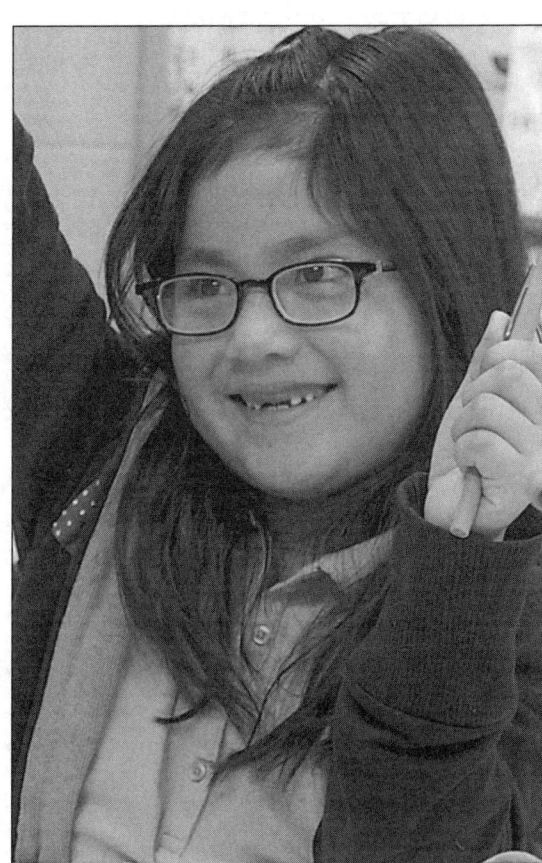

Reading and Role-Playing
Fairy Tales, Folktales, Fables, and Fantasy

RATIONALE/INTRODUCTION

In this unit, you'll invite your readers into the world of acting and directing, as well as the world of talking animals, heroes and heroines, fairies, princesses, and witches. There is a playful—yet vital—relationship between reading and drama. Consider the good and evil, quests and magic, chants and incantations. What fun children will have acting out the cackling witch or the wise, eccentric fairy godmother! When children read, they learn to embody the character, seeing through his or her eyes; they put themselves into the drama of the story, which allows them to understand it in richer ways, thinking about and considering the lessons these stories teach.

There are a number of reasons you may want to consider including this unit in your plans for the year. This is a unit designed for children reading levels J–M. If you teach first-graders who are mostly reading above the benchmark, then you may want to challenge them with this unit, which will involve reading books with rich literary language and vocabulary. This unit will build off of the character work you did in *Meeting Characters and Learning Lessons: A Study of Story Elements* (Unit 4), and will introduce them to new genres, as well as provide an opportunity for drama and fluency work, critical thinking, and richer conversations about books.

You might also consider this unit if after teaching your second-graders *Series Book Clubs* (Unit 4), you find that they could use more experience with a variety of genres, or that they could benefit from a focus on reading with drama and expression. Often, when children have been reading extensively in just a few series, they aren't getting as much practice with a range of authors' styles, and different types of stories. Though there are many benefits of series reading, you may find that after lots and lots of it, students might benefit from some practice with starting fresh books where the characters are brand-new and the setting is not familiar. You might also turn to this unit for support with teaching kids to think more deeply about the lessons in stories, and to think critically about the books they read.

In this unit, children will work in both partnerships and clubs. In both contexts, children will rely on the speaking and listening skills they have developed across the year, and they will also extend these skills. They will need to collaborate with increasing focus in order to co-direct and act out dramatic versions of their books. This means figuring out, together, how to convey what characters are thinking and feeling, how they hold themselves, what their facial expressions reveal—thinking about traits, points of view, how characters respond to big events and challenges, empathizing, synthesizing, making predictions, determining meaning, lessons and messages, and so forth. Children will need to ask clarifying questions, build on one another's ideas, make compromises, and consider new possibilities.

Because children will be thinking comparatively (across multiple versions of the same story, archetypes, viewpoints, and so on) during this unit, they will especially need to rely on analytical skills. As you plan your instruction for this unit, then, consider what you have taught in prior units, and how you can build on that work in ways that deepen and extend children's reading skills and comprehension.

ASSESSMENT

If you are selecting this particular unit of study, it is likely that your students already have some strategies under their belt for getting to know characters and are ready to transfer those strategies to a wider range of genres. You might want to look over your conferring notes and other observations to get a sense of how well children are still using those strategies that you taught in previous units.

Before diving into the unit, you can collect some more current assessment data that you can use to tailor your plans for the unit, especially if some time has passed since your last character unit. As in other units, you might use your students' responses to read-aloud as a tool for collecting data. Select a rich, engaging fairy tale to read aloud, one that contains all that you hope to teach into during the course of the unit: clear story structure, magical elements, literary language, archetypal characters, and a moral or lesson at the end. Then plan strategic places in the text to stop during your read-aloud.

When you come to a particularly vivid description of the setting, you may want to read it without showing the pictures. Then prompt students to jot or sketch what they are picturing in their mind, as an assessment of the envisioning work that you plan to teach in Bend I. You might also prompt for character feelings or the lessons the story might contain. Students will jot their responses on Post-its, which you can then collect and sort into groupings based on patterns that appear in their responses.

Your conferring notes and ongoing running records will also help you to uncover how much support your students will need with the literary language and vocabulary that they will encounter in fairy tales, folktales, fables, and fantasy. Look for patterns that reveal what students *are* doing when they encounter unfamiliar language: are they making substitutions that make sense, do they pause for a long time to think, do they skip words or phrases, omitting things completely? Looking for patterns and tendencies across your class will help you tailor that bend in the road to suit your students' needs.

A SUMMARY OF THE BENDS IN THE ROAD FOR THIS UNIT

Essential Question: How can I combine reading with role-playing and directing to grow my understanding of characters across fairy tales, folktales, fables, and fantasy?

- **Bend I: Stepping into the Magical World of Fairy Tales, Folktales, Fables, and Fantasy**

  How do I step into the world of the story, walking in different characters' shoes, feeling, thinking, and acting as they do, in order to gain a deeper understanding of who they are? How can my partner and I direct each other in the roles of characters in order to get a "big picture" view of all the story elements in our books, including the setting and magical elements?

- **Bend II: Literary Language and Vocabulary**

  How can I make sense of the complex language and literary devices common to the genres of fairy tales, folktales, fables and fantasy? How can I incorporate this language into my own vocabulary?

- **Bend III: Discovering Predictable Roles Characters Play**

  How can I think across the books I've been reading to grow my thinking about the predictable roles characters play, in fairy tales, folktales, fables, and fantasy?

- **Bend IV: Comparing and Contrasting Lessons That Stories Convey**

  How can my reading club work together to consider the lessons characters learn and to compare how different authors explore similar morals in sometimes very different ways?

In Bend I (Stepping into the Magical World of Fairy Tales, Folktales, Fables, and Fantasy), the invitation to become actors and directors may seem like play to children, but it will kick off a unit of serious work. As they reenact, students will read closely, stepping into the shoes of the characters in their stories, inferring how characters feel, and working with reading partners to envision the world of the story. Plan to spend a little over a week in this bend.

In Bend II (Literary Language and Vocabulary), children will spend a little over a week exploring various types of literary language, discussing and making meaning of the language they encounter with partners. As students dive into these genres, they'll be confronted with complex language, including figurative language, idioms and expressions, and also vocabulary typical of the genres. Often these stories include made-up words and wordplay, adding an extra challenge for readers.

In Bend III (Discovering Predictable Roles Characters Play), children will consider some predictable roles characters fall into, in fairy tales, folktales, fables, and fantasy, as well as in realistic fiction stories. They'll spend about a week thinking, too, about times when characters are more complicated, for examples when the villain redeems herself. Learning to seek archetypes and, on the other hand, to find complexity in characters, will help them as they read and study all kinds of literature.

In Bend IV (Comparing and Contrasting Lessons That Stories Convey), the focus is on the lessons stories can offer through what befalls characters. Children will use their best critical-thinking skills to determine not only some messages that readers can take away from each story but also whether these lessons are ones with which they themselves agree. They'll read across stories with similar themes or messages, considering similarities and differences across the books they read. It will take you about a week to wrap up the unit.

GETTING READY

Assemble a variety of fairy tales, folktales, fables, and fantasy.

This unit asks you to dust off your old books by the Brothers Grimm and Hans Christian Andersen. Bring out the wicked witches, enchanted princesses, and talking animals. Read aloud your favorites to children, and throw in the drama as you do! Gather up classic versions as well as adaptations and modern versions. Look for books that are "fairy-tale-ish," that is, books that contain even just some elements of fairy tales, folktales, or fables. Many early chapter-book fantasy series will contain the same story elements and character types that will be studied in this unit (*Magic Treehouse* by Mary Pope Osborne, *Secrets of Droon* by Tony Abbott, *Ricky Ricotta* by Dav Pilkey, and *Rainbow Magic* by Daisy Meadows, to name a few). To prepare for this unit, you will want to create an enticing new section in your classroom library just for fairy tales, folktales, fables, and fantasy.

Once you've organized baskets of fairy tales, folktales, fables, and fantasy, you can decide if you have enough books for each student to fill their baggie with just these books, or if you'll need to supplement with realistic fiction. Of course, if you can steer kids toward any realistic fiction books that contain characters that resemble archetypes found in fairy tales, you'll want to do so. In the Henry and Mudge series by Cynthia Rylant, for example, kids might say Henry solves problems a bit like a hero, and Mudge is like his sidekick. In the Mercy Watson series by Kate DiCamillo, Eugenia Lincoln could be considered a sort of villain, while Mercy often gets the credit for being the heroine (even when she really isn't). Realistic fiction will allow kids to be able to think critically about what really counts as a hero or villain as they read. Compared to the heroes and villains in most fairy tales, their realistic fiction books will contain characters that are probably more nuanced. Reading fairy tales and folktales alongside modern-day realistic fiction and other stories will also allow your children to compare and contrast, a skill that global standards spotlight and that is essential to becoming a more sophisticated reader and thinker.

Gather relevant anchor charts from previous units.

This unit is much like a character unit with a slant toward deeper comprehension work. You will want to read through all your anchor charts from previous units and gather up any that focus on thinking about characters, talking about books in partners or groups, dramatizing or acting parts out, jotting or sketching ideas about books, comprehension work, text support, or elaborating on ideas about books. You might display these in your meeting area, particularly near the start of the unit, when a few of the suggested minilessons will encourage kids to use everything they already know to put themselves in characters' shoes. When you can provide visual support for previous learning, you do students a huge favor (and yourself, as their teacher), making it much easier for them to utilize *all* that you have taught them.

Select the books you'll read aloud.

There are hundreds of classic fairy tales or folktales to pick from, as well as modern variations of these tales. You may want to choose two or three fairy tales and read multiple versions, beginning with a simple classic version, then reading more complex versions, and finally adaptations. For example, you might begin with James Marshall's *Cinderella*, then move to Marcia Brown's more complex version, then go to *Prince Cinders* by Babette Cole, then *The Paper Bag Princess* by Robert Munsch, perhaps ending with a story that is not technically a fairy tale at all but a realistic fiction story, like *Violet the Pilot* by Steve Breen. Or, you might decide to read a wide number or classic fairy tales, folktales, and fables, beginning with those that are somewhat familiar to your students and adding on lesser-known stories. Think about your particular class of students and then select titles that will capture their imagination. Throughout this unit, you will want to invite children to act out portions of the books you read aloud, which will then launch them into livelier, richer conversations about character.

Because this unit involves multiple genres, you will want to make a plan to read aloud at least one example of each to highlight the unique characteristics. Choose a fairy tale, a folktale, a fable, and an example of a fantasy story, like *Imogene's Antlers* by David Small or *Uni the Unicorn* by Amy Krouse Rosenthal, or *Dream Animals* by Emily Winfield Martin. You might decide to create a chart listing examples of each text type you've read aloud, and invite children to add the titles of their independent books to the chart as well. At the end of the unit, you may decide to celebrate with a mini-inquiry where students explore the differences between the genres and then present their findings.

Plan to establish book clubs in in the third bend of the unit.

We suggest that you devote the first portion of the unit to partnerships, in which children can practice acting out their books, and then, in Bend III, transition children to book clubs, to extend this work. In the third bend, you might form the clubs by simply combining two partnerships into groups of four. This is supportive for students, since they will already have had practice working together with their partner, and will simply be adding two more people to the group. On the other hand, you may wish to separate some of the partnerships, assigning some students to new groupings for various reasons: perhaps their reading levels have changed, or they might benefit from a new mix of people to work with. Maybe some children will benefit from reading in a group that is reading books a level or two easier (for fluency or other reasons), while others might benefit from being a part of a group that is reading at his or her instructional level. Club meetings will take the place of partnerships and will last just five or ten minutes a day, so as not to encroach on independent reading time.

For children who may need extra support, you will want to match them up in same-book partnerships, so that they can read the same books, talk about the same characters, and act out the same stories together. It will be much more challenging to do this work with a partner who is reading a different book. It may be that one child is able to read at a slightly higher level, but reads some easier books to share in this partnership.

BEND I: STEPPING INTO THE MAGICAL WORLD OF FAIRY TALES, FOLKTALES, FABLES, AND FANTASY

Invite children to bring books to life by role-playing the characters.

There is much to love about this unit. First, there are the books: many familiar tales, filled with magic and adventure, rich literary language, and much to think and talk about. Then, there is the drama. Your students will walk in the shoes of Goldilocks and Cinderella, of Little Red Riding Hood, and the Troll under the bridge. They'll role-play their books, putting on mini-performances daily. On the surface, your classroom will be filled with laughter and play and drama, complete with silly voices and funny gestures. But look a little deeper and it will be clear that your kids will be engaged in very high-level thinking: analyzing author's craft, thinking deeply and critically about characters, comparing and contrasting stories and the lessons contained within them.

Like many units, you'll want to start with what is familiar and build on that, introducing increasingly complex and sophisticated work as the unit progresses. In this unit, you'll launch with a focus on character work, which students will likely have had some practice with during past units. You might announce, "Over the next few weeks, you won't just talk about characters; you'll get to *be* them! You'll continue to read realistic fiction stories, but you'll also read fairy tales, folktales, fables, and fantasy. You'll have time every day to act these stories out with your reading partners, so get ready to be kings and queens, big bad wolves, and sly foxes, villains and heroes!"

Then, you can demonstrate and coach, using a dramatic excerpt from a familiar book, such as *The Three Little Pigs* by Paul Galdone, setting children up to reenact as they listen. Be dramatic as you read a page or two; make facial expressions, gesture with your hands and shoulders—your whole body if need be—and change your voice when each character speaks. Invite children to join you as actors, right from their spots in the meeting area.

You might say to the class, "How about if we try it—right here, right now? I'm going to reread the part when the wolf blows down the first pig's house. Partner 1, you'll be the wolf, and Partner 2, you'll be the Third Little Pig. Be the best hungry wolf you can be, eyeing that pig like it's your dinner. Be the best little pig you can be, shaking in your boots with fear. Use your face, your facial expressions, to show me what your characters are feeling. Big Bad Wolf, is your mouth watering as you imagine that delicious pig? Little Pig, are your eyes wide with fear as you wait for the Big Bad Wolf? What about your body? What are you doing with your arms? What about your nose? Ready? Wolves go ahead, *huff!* and *puff!*" After reading a page or so, reread again, this time with partners swapping roles, giving them a chance to see things from the other character's perspective.

Once children are warmed up, you'll turn their attention to the work that they'll do as readers, on their own, based on what you've just done as a class. Help them connect what they've done on this first day with what they'll be doing over the course of the unit and over the course of their reading lives. "Bravo!" you might say. "You are actors! When actors read their scripts, they close their eyes, and create a whole world in their mind. They walk in their characters' shoes, feeling what they feel, seeing what they see, doing what they do. You can read every story like actors! You might think to yourself, 'I bet she's really mad now' and then read the character's lines in an angry voice as you furrow your brow and scowl, or, 'I bet he's a little scared in this part,' and then cower a bit, and make a frightened face. And as you read, you'll pay attention to when a character's feelings might be changing and make sure that the voice in your head changes to show off that new feeling. Each of you will be doing this work on your own as you read, and later you'll have a chance to act it out with your partner. Putting yourself in the role of a character is one way that readers understand stories more deeply, one way they read more closely."

> **"Today I want to teach you that one way readers understand stories more deeply and read more closely is to put themselves into the role of a character. With a partner, you can reenact parts of a story, putting yourself in the characters' shoes. One person can explain how they're going to read the part and then read it and act it out. The other person, the listener, can give feedback."**

Before they enact their characters, readers can explain how they'll read the parts. For instance, a child might say, "I think in this part she is really sad because she was left behind, no one is with her, and she's also getting scared that she'll be deserted. So I think this part would sound like this." With your help, the listening partner will be able to talk back to the first reader, saying something like, "You said she was getting scared, but you gotta make her voice sound that way," and then will read the excerpt aloud to demonstrate. Partners can hold each other accountable to the book as well as to what they are trying to show in their enactments. Bear in mind that your goal for this unit is not only character work but also reading with fluency, prosody, and phrasing; reader's theater and repetitive reading make the world of difference.

Teach children to pay attention to a character's feelings to learn even more.

As they read on their own, teach children that they can mark places in their independent reading books where the main character has a strong feeling. Then, when they meet in partnerships, they can read aloud these passages to each other. They can use their voices and gestures as they read, so as to convey the range of emotion a character is experiencing. Reading with purpose and expression not only allows children to empathize with a character, it also supports accuracy and fluency. As partners talk, they may come up with different interpretations of the character's feelings. The listening partner may question her partner's idea that the character is excited. If so, that child could reread that part of the book, trying out a new facial expression or tone of voice, one she believes better represents the character's frame of mind.

> "Today I want to teach you that when you read you can always be aware of the places where the main character has strong feelings. You can mark these places so that later, you can read and act them out with your partner to better understand exactly how the character is feeling and what he or she might be experiencing."

You will likely need to teach your students to distinguish between shades of feelings; teach them to think about clues in the story that help to distinguish between when a character is content, for example, versus happy, versus elated. Often the text doesn't simply tell the reader how a character feels—instead readers have to use what is happening in the story to infer. One strategy for thinking more carefully about character feelings is to think of at least two or even three words to describe a character's feelings. This will help children describe more of the complexity of the characters, as well as build vocabulary for talking about characters in general. Instead of just saying *nervous*, by using two or three words, kids can say the character is feeling *nervous* and *anxious* and *worried*.

Read-aloud and shared reading are ideal times to pause and have discussions about how characters are feeling, and why. As you have these discussions, you may want to begin a vocabulary chart to display during this and other narrative units. As you add new feelings vocabulary, one word at a time, you can organize them by meaning—words that generally mean "happy" at one end of the scale, and words that mean "upset" or "angry" at the other end of the scale. This becomes a resource children can draw from during reading and writing times. Readers can pause to consider which words *did* the author choose and why? As writers, kids can refer to the chart and think, "Which words do *I* want to choose—and why?" When kids have a more expansive vocabulary for articulating how characters feel, this in turn gives them tools for expressing how they themselves feel.

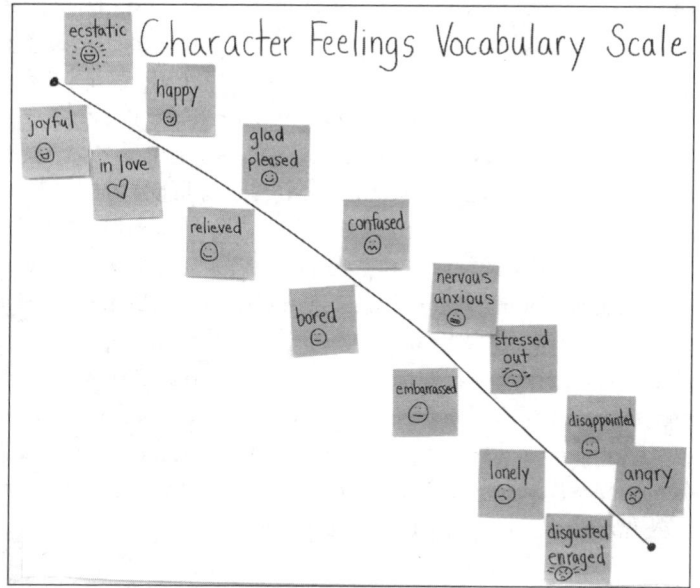

Challenge children to ask big questions about characters so as to come up with even bigger ideas.

Soon children will be ready for more sophisticated character work. You can teach them that once readers have identified strong feelings in a character, they analyze those feelings to understand more about that character. They ask themselves questions like, "Why does this character have this emotion?" They can also think about what that emotion says about the character. Do the feelings seem exaggerated? Is the character acting in ways that display his or her feelings, or trying to hide them? These are big questions, and you'll want to emphasize that readers look for answers. To do this, they reread, they look for clues, they pose theories, and they try out different possible interpretations. Encourage kids to cite evidence for the conclusions they draw about characters.

Teach students to envision the setting, the world of the story.

Launching students into fairy tales, folktales, fables, and fantasy with character work will feel familiar to you and your students. Chances are, you've already taught at least one character unit, so this will be a review of work that children have done before—albeit probably in easier books than the books they are reading now. Your next step, then, might be to teach students how to envision the magical worlds that their characters live in. Often, in fairy tales, folktales, fables, and fantasy, the worlds the characters live in are significantly different from the world we live in. You can teach your students that readers try to make a picture in their mind of that world—what does it look like, what does it feel like to live in that world, how is it the same and how is it different from the world we live in?

When students get together to act out their stories, they can practice narrating a little bit of "set up," describing the world where the story takes place. "Once upon a time," they might begin, "in a land . . ." This language will lead nicely into a description of where the story takes place. You might point out examples of fairy tales and other stories that begin with a bit of backstory—this often includes a summary of the place and time where the story is set, getting readers into the world of the story. Sometimes some of the key backstory information is contained within the illustrations. Children can begin their dramatizations by providing a backstory for their characters, using everything in the pictures and the words. After all, if writers of fairy tales often do this—why shouldn't actors too?

You might coach kids to elaborate on their descriptions of the setting through mid-workshop teaching, reminding students to pay attention to not just where the story takes place, but what time period and what time of day, among other details. More than that, what is the overall *feel* of the place? Teach students that settings, just like characters, often have a sort of personality of their own—is this a happy, innocent, picturesque countryside, or is this a darker, creepy, spooky forest? Of course, in some stories, especially higher-level books, the characters might move from one setting to another—think of *Three Billy Goats Gruff*—the goats live in the beautiful countryside, while the troll lives in a creepy underworld. Or think of *Magic Tree House*, how Jack and Annie live in the present, in a happy, safe, suburban neighborhood, but they travel to other, sometimes dangerous, worlds.

You'll also want to teach students to pay particular attention to the magic and other fantastical elements (imaginary creatures, talking animals and objects) of the books they are reading. Not only do these elements set these books apart from other fiction they have read, the magic is likely to play a key role in how characters relate to each other, how they deal with problems, and how the story unfolds. Readers need to be able to understand how the magic in a story works, and one way to understand it is to dramatize it. "Readers," you might say, "When's the last time you traveled in a spinning tree house, or cast a spell using your magic wand? What? You've never done those things in real life? Don't you want to try them out?" When students get together with partners, they can practice acting out the parts of the story that involve magic—not only are these the parts that are probably most interesting, they are probably also the parts that are more difficult to envision since readers can't rely very heavily on personal experience to picture what is happening.

You may want to begin a chart to list some of the kinds of magic kids are noticing in their books, as well as during read-aloud and shared reading. This needn't be an entire minilesson. Perhaps during a share or a mid-workshop teaching you might simply name out a few elements that have popped up in the books kids are reading:

Magic We've Discovered in Fairy Tales, Folktales, Fables, and Fantasy

- spells and curses
- talking animals
- coming back to life
- granting wishes

You'll add to this chart as time goes on, and eventually you may use it as a tool for comparing and contrasting different stories, asking children to think, "Do I know other stories that contain similar elements? What does that tell me about this new story I'm reading?"

Encourage children to capture their thinking by jotting.

As they read, students can use Post-its to capture their thoughts so that they can be better prepared to share their thinking with a partner. If your students have not been introduced to stopping and jotting, you might first practice during several read-alouds. You'll prepare your read-aloud ahead of time, marking a few key places for stopping and jotting—the same kinds of places you would usually stop and talk. Perhaps you'll choose places to stop and figure out how a character is feeling. You might say, "In today's read-aloud, you'll pay close attention to how the character feels, and you'll keep track of your thinking by jotting some words and phrases on Post-its." When you come to a preplanned spot in the text for stopping, you'll pause to coach children to write just a few words—not whole sentences for now. They may also need some tips on using abbreviations for names, and other time-savers, so that the notes they jot aren't taking too much time away from their reading.

After practicing a few jots on Post-its, you can prompt children to turn and talk with a partner, and use their notes to help their conversation. Jotting first lets them rehearse their partnership conversations, and it conveys to them that they are in charge of their own reading observations.

Once stopping and jotting on Post-its has been introduced during read-aloud time, then you may teach it as a strategy to be used during independent reading time. You might say, "Readers, just like we've been jotting notes during our read-alouds, you can jot some notes about your own books as well."

> "Today I want to teach you that one way readers preserve their thinking about stories is by jotting it down as it occurs, on Post-its. They can then use their Post-its as conversation starters when they discuss the passage later with their partner."

If your students are already familiar with a few strategies for stopping and jotting, remind them of the strategies they know. Bring out any charts you may have already created on ways to track a character's wants and troubles, and recall what children learned about marking books with Post-its, noting things to talk about with their partner. Tell them that actors, and readers, too, keep notes as a way to get inside a character's head and to put themselves into that role. Readers (and actors) are not only interested in how a character feels from scene to scene—but they want to figure out the character's overall personality as well. Remind them (if they have learned this in the past) that when readers see a pattern in the way a character acts, they have probably identified a trait of that character. You will probably want to leave the invitation to jot notes open ended, allowing children to choose when and how to jot, inventing their own strategies as they go.

As the unit continues, you can glance over a child's Post-its and glean a snapshot of what kind of work they have been doing as a reader. A child whose books are "feathered" with Post-its, too many in fact, is doing a lot of work as a reader, but may need some support with determining importance. "Wow! Look at all the great ideas you are having!" you might exclaim, counting up the scores of Post-its in one single book. "Let me teach you a strategy for figuring out when something is important enough to save on a Post-it . . ." You might then teach the child to notice just the key details, such as who the story is mostly about, where they are at each part of the story, what they are doing, and why they are doing it. Or perhaps you'll steer the child toward jotting just the parts where a character seems to be changing. Or perhaps just a Post-it for the beginning, middle, and end of the book, really requiring some decisions about what details are worthy of hanging on to, and what can be let go.

There might also be children whose books remain absent of Post-its. If the child reads books below level J or K, this might actually be preferable, so that the child is using every minute to read. If the child is reading early chapter books, you might then use your observations and running records to decide what kind of comprehension work the child needs to practice—then decide if Post-its are a tool that will help—or not.

Invite children to direct each other, in order to see the big picture.

As this first bend nears an end, you'll invite your children to step out of the character's shoes and to put on the hat of the director. "Readers, do you know what a director of a movie does? A director has to understand not just how *one* character feels but how *all* the characters feel. A director has to understand the setting, too, and how the plot twists and turns, and the ways in which all these components work together. Directors have to see the whole picture, the *whole story*."

Then issue an invitation: "Do you know what I think? I think all of you are ready to be directors. I've watched you these past few days and noticed how, even as you're watching your partner play the role of the bully, you're able to think through the whole story and say to your partner, 'I think she's more scared than that. Try putting your hands over your eyes and shaking a little.' That's *directing*! You're thinking about the whole story to help you understand the characters—and then you're giving each other little directions or cues to show that. For the next few days, we're each going to have a turn doing more of this big-picture, whole-story work." You may then wish to fishbowl two children playing the roles of actor and director to model this work.

In this final stretch of the bend, aim to lift the level of children's enactments and remind them that readers, like directors, pay attention not only to *what* and *why* a character does things but also to *how* the character does these things. Does the book give any clues about the character's gestures? About the way a character walks or sits or closes the door? If the book says that a character slumps in the chair, then we need to ask, "*Why* does she sit like that? Is she tired? Bored? What's going on?" Readers also pay attention to the way characters talk: the dialogue tags, the words they choose, their tone of voice, and the cues the author gives through dialogue. All of these give hints about what kind of people live in the world of a story. During read-aloud, perhaps you'll chart some of those clues:

Pay Attention to How Characters Act

- gestures
- the way a character moves
- dialogue tags
- word choice
- passages in the text that are explanations of characters' motives (reasons behind what they do)

Sometimes the author offers a window into a character's mind; he or she will write passages about a character's thinking or offer an explanation of a character's motives. Characters, like real people, have reasons behind what they do. They are motivated by feelings (jealousy, revenge, fear), situations, and relationships. Being a director means you are always filling in the gaps of a story as you read by drawing on all you learn from this book, from other books, and from your own life.

BEND II: LITERARY LANGUAGE AND VOCABULARY

Now your unit will take a slight turn. You've launched your classroom into the world of fairy tales, folktales, fables, and fantasy. Kids are dramatizing stories, changing their voices to match how characters feel, closing their eyes and imagining faraway lands. By now you may have noticed that many of the books that your children are reading contain language that is quite different from the language they use every day. Ask a kid, and they'll tell you that fairy-tale characters "talk fancy" or "old-fashioned." They cast spells using made-up words, and often speak in very complex sentences. In short, these books are filled with literary language.

You might launch this bend in the road by having students *listen* to some examples of professional storytelling. Sometimes hearing the sound of storytelling (versus reading it and having to give voice to it in our heads) helps clarify what we mean when we say storytelling language or literary language. "Today," you might say to your kids, "we're not going to just be actors—we're also going to become storytellers." Play an audio clip from professional storytellers like Heather Forest, Carmen Agra Deedy, or Lester Laminack (or even yourself!), and ask kids to name some of the things they notice these storytellers do with their voices. They will likely notice that these professional storytellers:

- use a singsongy type of voice
- are loud at some parts and soft at others
- use sound effects
- sometimes use long pauses
- match their voices to the mood of the story
- use different words than everyday language

You could remind kids that in writing workshop they've worked on becoming storytellers as well—they've learned to use descriptive details, comparisons, vivid imagery, and interesting sounds and patterns in their poetry and narrative writing. Just like the authors of the books they read. "Today, as you are reading and talking with your partners, practice using your best storytelling voices, just like what we just listened to."

Students often read right over literary language without stopping to appreciate it or even to understand it. You might teach students to notice places in their fairy tales, folktales, fables, or fantasy books where authors have used language in inventive, playful, or beautiful ways. If you teach second grade, your students will be familiar with this from the work they did in *Bigger Books Mean Amping Up Reading Power* (Unit 3).

> **"Today I want to teach you that sometimes authors use extra-special words, kind of like they are tugging on your shirtsleeve, saying 'Listen here!' Readers notice when an author has used extra-special words and make sure they understand what the author is trying to say or show."**

In the books kids are reading now, there are often inventive words that have to do with magic or fantasy—things that aren't real—so figuring out the meaning of those words poses an extra-special challenge. You can show students examples from the books they know, such as *Cinderella* by Marcia Brown. Ask them, "What words and phrases seem like extra-special storybook language to you? Why do you think the author used those words?"

The next night the two sisters were off again to the ball, and so was Cinderella, but this time even more splendidly dressed than before. The prince never left her side. All evening he paid her charming compliments. The young miss found this so far from boring that she forgot her godmother's warning. She was horrified to hear the first stroke of midnight before she thought it could be eleven o'clock. She rose and fled as lightly as a doe. The prince followed her, but he could not overtake her. In her haste, Cinderella dropped one of her glass slippers. The prince gathered it up with the greatest care.

In the example above, children might notice phrases like "splendidly dressed" and "The young miss found this so far from boring" or "fled as lightly as a doe." Of course, there aren't "correct" answers here about what can be defined as extra-special storybook language—what is important is that children will surmise why the author decided to say "splendidly dressed" instead of just "fancy," or why she wrote "as lightly as a doe" instead of just "quickly." You can coach children to develop theories about the choices the writer made, how the writer created a voice or a style, and how other fairy tales and classic tales have similar, yet different voices.

Next, you might focus in on more specific types of literary language, such as similes and comparisons. Demonstrate using a passage from a book where an author has described something by suggesting it is like something else that is actually *very* different. Show kids how the author expects readers to bring those two distinct things together based on how they are alike in ways that create a brand-new, made-for-the-moment meaning. This strategy will be familiar to second-graders from Unit 3 (but new to first-graders). Of course, if you have taught students to add comparisons to their own poems or stories, this will be a natural extension.

> **"Readers, today I want to teach you that sometimes, an author will compare two things that are *very* different. As a reader, you have to stop and think, 'How are these two things alike? What is the author trying to say? What would make sense for the story?'"**

Again, you can demonstrate this using examples from familiar books, such as *Cinderella* by James Marshall:

On the day of the ball,
Cinderella was exhausted from trying
to make her stepsisters look beautiful.
"Wouldn't **you** like to go to the ball?"
they said, teasing her cruelly.
"Oh yes!" said Cinderella.
"Don't be ridiculous!" cried the stepsisters.
"What would a wretched mouse like you
do at a fancy ball?"
And they shrieked with laughter.

With your support, children will see that the stepsisters, of course, didn't mean that Cinderella is literally a mouse, or even that she looks like a mouse. Coach and demonstrate how to use the context, the parts that come before and after the phrase, to figure out what "wretched mouse" means in *this* passage. "Whenever you are reading," you might say, "you can be on the lookout for comparisons, or similes. Think to yourself, what does comparison really mean? How are these two different things alike?" You can invite children to use comparisons when they are talking about their books with their reading partners, incorporating figurative language into their own ways of talking about books.

In fairy tales, folktales, fables, and fantasy, it is not unusual for authors to include wordplay—especially in adaptations to the classics. Think of "Dogerella" and her fairy "Dogmother." That's pretty funny—to a kid who "gets" the wordplay. Or the moral to the song Little Bunny Foo Foo: "Hare today, goon tomorrow!" The morals to many of Aesop's fables involve a little idiom, or expression, that is meant to be clever, but also instructive: "Beware of a wolf in sheep's clothing." In a minilesson you can teach students that when they come across particularly tricky literary language that involves playing with words, they may need to do a bit of extra thinking to figure out what is meant. Demonstrate reading from a passage that isn't particularly tricky to decode, but leaves room for figuring out the meaning of a play on words.

Authors might play around with words that can mean different things, and sometimes they intend a meaning readers don't expect. When authors do that, readers can stop and think, "Wait a minute! That's not what it *really* means!" Then they use what's happening in the story to think about what would make sense. You might step outside of fairy tales, folktales, fables, and fantasy to give examples, from joke books or Amelia Bedelia, showing a range of examples of this type of playful language. Some children, being very literal, will need to be vigilant, and on the lookout for language like this, using a special "radar" for wordplay.

> **"Today I want to teach you that authors sometimes use playful language or words that can mean different things. It is up to the reader to use what's happening in the story and think about what would make sense, to figure out what the author meant."**

Fairy tales, folktales, fables, and fantasy often include vocabulary that is special to the genre. These books are filled with kings and queens, but also lords and butlers and heirs to the throne, carriages and footmen, balls, galas, unicorns, ogres, and grandfather clocks. It's easy, as an adult, to take these seemingly simple words for granted—but this is specialized vocabulary. Combine this with the often-complex sentence structure where these words are found, and kids are in for quite a challenge! You'll want to teach a strategy or two for figuring out these words. "When you come to a tricky word," you might say to your kids, "one thing you can do is look across the whole word and break the word apart into parts you know. Then push all the parts back together to say the whole word." Make a word like *unicorn* with magnetic letters, and move the letters apart to show "uni" (a prefix they've likely seen by now) and "corn" (a familiar, easy-to-decode word for kids at this level). Point to "uni" and "corn" separately a few times to demonstrate breaking the word apart, and then push the magnetic letters back together and say the word smoothly, *unicorn*, to demonstrate putting it all back together again.

You'll also want to remind children that figuring out how to say the word is not enough. Readers read all around the word, before and after, for clues hinting at what the word might mean. Sometimes readers cover up the tricky word with their finger and think, "What word or phrase would make sense here?" Sometimes we think, "Okay I don't know *exactly* what this word means, but I think know it has something to do with _____." Then, if they've tried everything, they can always mark the super-tricky words with a Post-it and show them to their reading partner to get help later.

Near the end of the bend, you can teach kids that it's not just the words that are tricky in fairy tales, folktales, fables, and fantasy—it's the sentences, too. Sometimes it's helpful to read longer, more complicated sentences in parts, breaking the sentence into smaller clusters of words, thinking about what each group of words means, and then rereading to put it all back together again. You might teach kids to look for signal words (like *if, or, but*) as places to break a sentence apart. Punctuation like commas and quotation marks for dialogue is also helpful for making sense of a longer sentence.

To wrap up the bend, you might teach a repertoire lesson, demonstrating how readers use *everything* in combination to make sense of their stories and read with drama and expression. You might refer back to all the qualities of professional storytelling they learned at the start of the bend and remind them that they too are actors and storytellers.

BEND III: DISCOVERING PREDICTABLE ROLES CHARACTERS PLAY

Move children from partnerships to book clubs of four students.

As children move from partnerships to clubs in this bend, not only will their foundational skills (fluency, word solving, and accuracy) be supported by book club discussion, but the additional (sometimes opposing) viewpoints will challenge them to think more critically about books and characters. Just as students were in the routine of sitting with their reading partner in the meeting area as well as at their reading spots, you'll now introduce new spots, assigned next to their clubmates. You might also make it a new routine to turn and talk as a club whenever possible, rather than just in partnerships—the more they practice speaking and listening in a group, the better their conversations will eventually be.

In this bend of the unit, children will learn to think categorically—and also critically—about characters. You'll introduce the idea that just as there are different personality types in the world, there are different character types in stories. One character type might be the good guy—the hero—while another is the bad guy—the villain. And then, of course, there's the sidekick, the wise adviser, and the trickster, to name just a few more.

Even early chapter books contain identifiable character types. Pairs of friends—Ivy and Bean, Eric and Cam, Annie and Jack—are common in books for this age, with one friend sometimes being a bit more mischievous or daring. The wise adviser will often be a teacher or a parent, though this role might be played by someone who does, in fact, resemble the archetypal quirky sage or fairy godmother—the character, Morgan le Fey, in the Magic Treehouse series by Mary Pope Osborne, for example. In this bend, you will build on the character work from throughout the year, but this time, through the lens of fairy tales and folktales. The identifiable character types still exist in these kinds of stories, but with the added magical element that these tales incorporate. The villain (the wicked witch, the evil stepmother) has some sort of malicious bent. The hero truly embodies goodness and often exhibits extreme cleverness, even in the face of difficult situations. The wise adviser is often a powerful, magical character, providing guidance, advice, or even some sort of magical gift to the hero. In this bend you will explore these common character archetypes and how they aid in comprehension.

Teach children to read on the lookout for different character types—noticing patterns and making predictions.

You might introduce the bend like this: "Readers, by now you know a lot about how authors put characters together; you know that authors give characters wants and struggles, and personality traits and feelings. Today I want to teach you that as readers come to know something about how characters are created, they start to realize that particular types of characters pop up in lots of different books—and they read on the lookout for these types."

Then to launch kids' work on character types in an engaging and memorable way, you might role-play several well-known archetypes. Perhaps you'll put on a simple hat or hold a prop and briefly impersonate each character type. Or perhaps you'll choose three or four students to do this for you. With two students holding a piece of fabric as your curtain, you might reach behind your easel and pull out a magic wand. When the students move the curtain aside, you might say (in your very best fairy godmother voice), "Hello! I'm your fairy godmother! I'm always kind and sweet and helpful. I often have magical powers—but sometimes I disguise myself as an ordinary person. Thumbs up if you've ever read a book with a fairy godmother or other character like me in it." Then ask your helpers to put the curtain back up, put on a witch's hat, and when the curtain drops you'll introduce yourself as the evil witch combined with an evil stepmom. "I'm often jealous of the hero or heroine, and I'm tricky. I might use a poison apple or an impossible riddle to trap my victims. Thumbs up if you've ever had a character like me in one of your books."

You might introduce one or two other common archetypes and then, for the active-engagement piece of the lesson, ask the kids to think of another. "When you've thought of another character type, give me a thumbs up . . . now get ready to pretend to be that character type." (If necessary, you could scaffold this work by listing several character archetypes on a sheet of chart paper and asking students to choose one from the list to work with.) Pause to give students a moment to prepare. Perhaps remind them that you are asking them to pretend to be a character *type*, not just a specific character. "You look ready. Turn and introduce yourself to your club members *as a character type*." You might end by asking children to draw and label villains, heroes and heroines, sidekicks, fairy godmothers, wise old sages, and other archetypes from books they have read so far. You might have kids do this work on index cards that you can then collect and use to create a chart. Children will have fun noticing the various iterations of the hero, the bad guy, the sidekick, and coming up with a list of the different roles their characters play. The chart can also serve as a visual reminder of some of the character types to be on the lookout for as students read these tales.

This thinking across books categorically and analytically is sophisticated work. Children can work together to consider what it means to be one kind of character or another. Are there typical patterns of behavior they observe in certain character types? They might, for example, notice that the main character's sidekick is sometimes funny—that that person's role is to crack jokes. Or maybe the sidekick (or one of a pair of friends) tends to get the main character into trouble over and over—he is a troublemaker.

Earlier in the year, your children will have learned that characters in stories encounter trouble. Now they might notice that friends sometimes contribute to that trouble. Alternatively, the person who creates obstacles for the main character may be someone with a deliberate villainous intent—the class bully, for example, or the mean kid next door, the sly fox who attempts to trick the Gingerbread Man, or Cinderella's jealous stepsisters. To think in their clubs about how these roles play out in their books, students can act out scenes that spotlight the bully or the sidekick or the quirky adviser. As they did in the first bend, children can consider their various interpretations of these character types, perhaps trying the enactment through one child's perspective and then another's.

Children can also consider the role a character plays in order to predict what's going to happen and to detect patterns. Is the character good or bad? Will she win or will she lose? Why is this happening? What will happen next? They can also think about whether a character is the one who is teaching a lesson or learning one. You'll return to this in greater detail in the final bend of the unit. For now, it's enough to nudge children to read with an eye toward it.

> **"Today I want to teach you that readers consider the role of each character as they predict what's going to happen next. They might think, 'Who is the hero and who is the villain?' and 'What does this make me think about who will win and who will lose or what will happen next?'"**

Teach children to recognize character types—and their roots in old moralistic tales.

Now is the perfect time to use read-aloud to spotlight that the character types children encounter in their modern-day stories have roots in fairy tales, folktales, and fables. These short moralistic tales are particularly powerful teaching texts in part because they feature characters who have such clearly defined, often exaggerated traits. Children will have an easy time identifying the heroes and heroines, and the villains in these stories—and eventually, other archetypes, too. These tales are full of drama, so when you read them aloud—as we suggest you do—be sure to throw some gestures into your performance and give characters distinguishable voices to spotlight the role each one plays. Cackle and act crotchety as the wicked old witch; make your voice light and sweet when you are the hero or the heroine. Meanwhile, encourage your kids to ham it up too, as they step into these roles. "Fee, Fi, Fo, Fum!" demands to be spoken in a loud, mean voice. "Mirror, Mirror on the wall, who's the fairest of them all?" will sound more cunning and coy—and will have a singsong quality. Fairy tales, folktales, and fables (which originated as oral stories) are full of repetitive chants that students will love to perform. Meanwhile, these repeated lines supply both rhythm and meaning in a story.

Set children up to compare and contrast different versions of the same story and to explore authors' varying viewpoints.

Beyond simply enjoying the drama and aurally pleasing nature of these tales, your students will need to read them critically, thinking across messages, across authorial intent. You will want students to carry what they know about character types from one story to the next as they continue to read. This is integral work to becoming more sophisticated readers and thinkers. After children have heard several tales, they will begin to recognize similar characters—a bad wolf, a wise old man, an evil step relation. You can teach them that once readers recognize recurring types of characters, they can be on the lookout for them—quickly predicting more about a character and their role in the story. Will this be a wise elder who has all the answers but makes the main character work to get them? Will it be an evil stepmother who goes out of her way to harm the heroine? Will this be the obedient, loyal, kind third child of a royal family who will win in the end?

Once children recognize an archetype, you might point out that these archetypes differ somewhat from story to story. For example, the wolf in *Little Red Riding Hood* and *The Three Little Pigs* is the villain in both stories, but the wolf in the first story is often craftier than the wolf in the latter. Both Cinderella and Snow White feature evil stepmothers, but Cinderella's stepmother, whose motivation is to secure the prince for one of her own daughters, operates on a much less sinister level than Snow White's stepmother, who is so jealous of Snow White that she is out to kill her. Kids will revel in comparing and contrasting these archetypical characters!

Kids will encounter versions of these archetypes again and again in their modern-day reading, albeit in nonmagical forms. Children might observe, "Instead of a wolf, this book has Mean Jean the Recess Queen." And, as their books become more complex, they will come across characters who aren't strictly good or bad but a blend of both: heroes who begin weak and end up strong, kids who are sometimes nice and sometimes mean, villains who redeem themselves by the book's end.

> **"Today I want to teach you that when readers encounter a character type in a new book, they often think back on other books with the same character type. Readers ask themselves, 'How is this new character the same as and different from the characters in other books I have read?' This often leads to ideas and questions that are interesting to talk about with a book club."**

Invite your children to do some critical thinking.

Fairy tales and folktales can sometimes send stereotyped or antiquated messages to children, so be sure to use this opportunity to teach strategies for critical literacy. Read aloud updated versions of fairy tales that young children will relate to, tales that combat stereotypes in very obvious ways. *The Paper Bag Princess* by Robert Munsch and *Not All Princesses Dress in Pink* by Jane Yolen are two examples of children's books that very clearly defy stereotypical representations of girls. *William's Doll* by Charlotte Zolotow or *Oliver Button Is a Sissy* by Tomie dePaola helps kids understand and think of alternatives to stereotypical representations of boys.

You can emphasize that while fairy tales often include character types who are one-dimensional, in real life people are much more complicated. You might discuss how people are not "all one way." In real life, people might not be what they seem at first impression. They can have multiple sides to their personality, strengths and weaknesses, good and bad. Meanwhile, the evil characters in fairy tales are often just as ugly on the outside as they are on the inside, while the heroes and heroines are often beautiful and perfect in every way. Even young children understand that real people have more than one side to their personality.

You might also invite kids to think about and name what groups of people are actually represented in the pages of the classic versions of fairy tales, fables, and folktales. They may notice (or if not, you might model noticing) there are girls, boys, rich, poor, strong, weak, beautiful, not-so-beautiful, and yes—for those literal thinkers—there are animals represented too. Kids may also realize there are groups that are noticeably absent—especially if you think about the people who never get to be the hero or heroine. Where are all the people of color? Where are people who speak another language? Where are girls that don't dress in fancy dresses? Where are people that live in big cities? What about people from other countries? What about grandmas and grandpas, elderly folks—why aren't they ever the heroes or heroines? Invite kids to always be on the search for who might be missing, and as they begin to realize that this doesn't really seem very fair, then they might imagine and talk, in their book clubs, about versions of the story that are more inclusive.

> **"Today I want to teach you that you can always imagine new versions of fairy tales, folktales, and fables (or any book!), where there are more groups of people represented in the story. In your clubs, you can tell new versions of the stories you've read, changing the characters to make the story include groups of people that you haven't seen much in your books."**

Then, of course, be sure that you read aloud and make more inclusive versions of these tales available. Include texts that showcase many viewpoints and perspectives, as well as versions from around the world. Make these front and center alongside the classic versions in your classroom.

BEND IV: COMPARING AND CONTRASTING LESSONS THAT STORIES CONVEY

Examine characters' motivations to uncover lessons.

During the final bend of this unit, children will learn to unearth the lessons and messages stories convey. Fairy tales, folktales, and fables anchor this teaching, because they usually contain messages close to the surface of the story—messages such as greed, jealousy, and revenge lead to misfortune, and that working hard, taking risks, and standing up for the underdog are worthy causes.

Of course, the characters in modern-day children's literature face obstacles and learn lessons, just as the Three Pigs and Cinderella and countless other characters in these age-old folktales and fairy tales do. You can teach children to read both ancient and modern literature through this lens, identifying both characters' motivations and actions, and what happened in the story as a result of these actions.

This examination of the actions characters take and the consequences that befall them as a result, is a natural segue into a discussion of the lessons readers can take away from stories. You might initiate the conversation with a read-aloud, asking children what they think the stories teach. Fables often feature two differing approaches to life, so they are a perfect vehicle for children to investigate point of view. You might hold a debate in which half the room takes the viewpoint of the tortoise (in *The Tortoise and the Hare*), the other half, the hare. Ask children to engage in a little debate, thinking about why a particular character looks at things one way and to defend that character's viewpoint. Which point of view pays off in the story? What lesson does that point to? Because fables are short, different points of view could also be explored through role-play and small performances.

Spotlight how to recognize patterns and uncover important lessons.

Before long, students will recognize patterns in the lessons they are uncovering: good triumphs over evil, bad things happen to selfish or lazy characters. Teach children that determining a lesson to learn from the story is part of reading it, and that readers find lessons by taking note of what characters do that leads to trouble, and not doing that. Or, by taking note of what a character does when things do go well and using that to guide their behavior.

> "Today I want to teach you that readers learn lessons from the books they read. One way they can do this is by noticing what behaviors or actions contribute to a character's trouble and avoiding those behaviors in their own lives, or taking note of what kinds of things bring success, and using it to guide their own behavior."

For example, you might retell the familiar tale of the Three Little Pigs and then ask the class, "What did some of the little pigs do that did not go well for them?" Give students a moment to talk in their clubs, and then push them further by asking them to think outside the text, to their own lives. "So, what should *we* not do if we agree with the lesson of this story? What can we learn, that we can take to our own lives, our own experiences, based on what actions caused problems for the little pigs?" Continue on, asking students to then reflect on what lead to success for the third little pig. "What went well for that third little pig? And what does that mean we should do, according to the tale? How can we make that lesson apply to our everyday lives (and I don't just mean building houses out of certain materials)?" You might have to offer up some examples, extrapolating step by step and landing at: "In *The Three Little Pigs* we learn to avoid flimsy solutions." You might also teach children that readers look beyond the most obvious lesson—or the one spelled out at the end—to consider other more subtle lessons. Perhaps we can learn from the wolf's eventual death that "Sometimes, it's best to just take 'no' for an answer."

As children continue to read the fairy tales, folktales, fables, and fantasy in their book baggies, as well as their realistic fiction books, they'll hunt for lessons and morals to the stories. You'll remind them (as they will have learned in prior character units), nearly all stories contain lessons, and it is their job as readers to uncover and think through those lessons. They might align Post-its from fairy tales, folktales, fables, and fantasy they've read with ones they've written about similar passages in their realistic fiction books, noting the various ways in which authors of these different kinds of stories explore similar topics.

Children can consider what they themselves can learn from characters' motives, words, and actions. After reading Mo Willems's *I Love My New Toy!* for example, you might ask, "What can we learn from Piggie, who got so angry at Gerald?" Then say, "When we get angry and jump to conclusions, we may hurt our friends' feelings. Sometimes it's hard to do, but hearing our friends out and accepting their apologies preserves a friendship." Then you might teach children that readers can learn alongside the characters in these tales, imagining how they might live their own lives differently because of what the characters have learned, thus applying what they are learning during reading workshop to other contexts.

> **"Today I want to teach you that readers learn alongside the characters in their books. One way they might do this is by imagining how they will live their own lives differently because of what the characters have learned."**

Of course, some tales teach lessons with which you and your students don't agree. As in Bend III, you'll want to encourage your students to do some critical thinking. Readers can work in their clubs to think about whether a lesson doesn't ring true in their own world. Perhaps they'll notice, for example, that many fairy tales end with the prince and the princess living "happily ever after" or that the good guy always wins, and they might point out that this is not always true in life. Additionally, the modern-day stories they read may not have such happily-ever-after endings, though they may nonetheless end on a positive note. Readers can ask themselves, "Do I agree with it?" or "Does the good guy always win?" or "Was that the best way to teach the lesson?" or "Do I believe this is a good way to live my own life?"

Here you have an opportunity to present modern-day takes of classic tales, such as *The True Story of the 3 Little Pigs*, by Jon Scieszka (you launched the unit by reading aloud Paul Galdone's version of the tale). You might engage children in an inquiry in which they consider the question: "Why might this author have rewritten this story? What lessons might he be trying to convey?" Oftentimes, you'll find that in addition to having a little fun, authors like Jon Scieszka are out to challenge outdated views by presenting the other side. It may seem outrageous that the wolf could be considered anything but the villain, until you read his version of the story and realize that he is in fact only acting according to his nature; a wolf does eat pigs, after all. This might provide a good opportunity to discuss the concept of stereotypes.

Children will love the humor present in these modern-day versions, and will meanwhile engage in some lively debates about human (or wolf) nature, identity, motivations, and so forth. You could even set up a formal debate in which some children defend the wolf and others challenge him—or in which children argue the merits of the original tale versus those of the newer version. Challenge them to back up their arguments with text evidence, as well as real-life experience. This will strengthen their character analysis skills and hone their close-reading skills.

Create categories of books that go together.

To further promote this cross-text thinking, you might read aloud fables, fairy tales, and folktales that convey lessons similar to ones children have encountered in the realistic fiction books they've read, or those that you've read aloud. Ask children to think about how different authors convey the same lesson, or how different authors have opposing views on things. Many children's books mirror these old tales, so it could be nice work for the class to make bins of old and new books that go together. If you have multiple versions of *Cinderella* told by writers from around the world, those might all go into the same bin. Modern versions (*Cinder Edna* by Ellen Jackson and *Cinder-Elly* by Frances Minters are favorites) might go in that bin too, as could realistic fiction and other books with similar themes and lessons such as *Rosie Revere, Engineer* by Andrea Beaty, or *Oliver Button Is a Sissy* by Tomie dePaola (the characters in these books are ostracized in the beginning, but triumph in the end, just like Cinderella). Children will enjoy thinking across the differences among these tales. Have fun with these groupings, but don't force them. If you and your kids don't find ways to match new books with traditional tales, come up with new categories: "books about friends that help each other" or "books about kids who save the day."

Children can also create book baskets based on the lessons and morals books convey. They can discuss how books with similar lessons are the same and different. Club members can then work together to challenge one another's category choices and consider other baskets that might be more appropriate. Club mates can defend their ideas based on the evidence they have gathered in their books. They can also entice each other to read the book and the evidence of a suggested theme or moral. They will monitor and question each other, saying things like, "Why do you think it should go there?" or "Did you ever think maybe it is really about ____?"

> **"Today I want to teach you that readers often think about books that go together: books that are versions of the same story, books that teach the same lessons, books that contain similar character types. Book clubs can work together to take all the books they've read and sort them into bins of books that go together. That way, other readers can find many books that they might be interested in, just by going to one basket or section of the library."**

As children read several books that go together, teach them the importance of rereading. Often, we spend the first read focusing largely on the literal happenings; then, when we reread, we make more inferences and interpretations. The goal, of course, is that your readers think and talk *across* books, noting similarities that exist on many levels. By inviting children to help reorganize the library and to think about new book baskets, you open up more opportunities for them to think and apply and extrapolate to other contexts what they've learned.

CELEBRATION

As this unit draws to a close, you might end your study with a mini-inquiry, gathering your class together during a minilesson and asking "Now that we've read quite a few of these books, really studying the characters and the worlds they live in, what would you say is the difference between fairy tales, folktales, fables, and fantasy?" By the end of this unit, your students will have had experiences with all four genres through read-aloud and shared reading, as well as through independent reading.

You might start by demonstrating your own thinking about one or two favorite tales, giving reasons why you categorize Sleeping Beauty as a fairy tale, and Three Billy Goats Gruff as a folktale, for example. Then invite children to try this with a few other stories. Children might say, "I think Cinderella is a fairy tale, because it has magic, and a princess, and a happy ending." Another child might pipe up and say, "But not all fairy tales have princesses. What about The Three Little Pigs?" Yet another student might add, "But I think Three Little Pigs is not a fairy tale—maybe it's a folktale?" Keep in mind that many folktales can also be considered fairy tales, and vice versa. There is much overlap in the defining characteristics of each genre; what matters here is that students are exploring the books and coming up with their own classifications, which they can then explain and defend.

Rather than wrapping things up neatly with a concrete yes or no, leave children with open minds, ready to go off and search their book baggies with a stance toward questioning, rather than certainty. With their clubs, they can do their best to identify the genre of each of the books in their baggies, using everything they have learned about characters, setting, language, and theme to provide examples and reasons for why they believe each book should be labeled as a particular genre. Kids can create stacks of each genre, noticing what is the same and what is different about each. The covers of some books will likely provide clues (some declare themselves folktales or fables), there are sure to be books that cross genres, and there are likely to be questions that even you don't have the answers to! The truth is, all four genres share many characteristics, and while some books may be clearly labeled "fairy tale" or "folktale" or "fable" or "fantasy," there will be inevitable overlap. Even under the category "fantasy" there are subgenres—high fantasy, low fantasy, science fiction, and superheroes to name a few—that are sure to be found in your classroom library.

More important than any label or category, is that children are learning to enter into the world of the story—especially stories that take place long ago and far away, in magical lands far different from the world we live in. After sorting books into piles of fairy tale(ish), folktale(ish), fable(ish), and fantasy(ish), you might wrap up the celebration by reading aloud one of your students' favorite stories, one last time, inviting students to take on the roles of various characters, perhaps with one or two students taking on the roles of directors. Perhaps you'll video-record this time, preserving their favorite story to post on your class blog to watch with families at home, or during inside recess at school, or to leave playing in the school library as a sort of digital display of your students' work.

BEND I: STEPPING INTO THE MAGICAL WORLD OF FAIRY TALES, FOLKTALES, FABLES, AND FANTASY

- "Today I want to teach you that one way readers understand stories more deeply and read more closely is to put themselves into the role of a character. With a partner, you can reenact parts of a story, putting yourself in the characters' shoes. One person can explain how they're going to read the part and then read it and act it out. The other person, the listener, can give feedback."

- "Today I want to teach you that when you read you can always be aware of the places where the main character has strong feelings. You can mark these places so that later, you can read and act them out with your partner to better understand exactly how the character is feeling and what he or she might be experiencing."

- "Today I want to teach you that characters can experience different shades, or degrees of feelings, and often the author never comes right out and tells you exactly how the character feels. Readers can use clues from what is happening in the story to figure out exactly how a character feels: not just 'happy' or 'sad.' One way to be more precise when you talk to your partners about character feelings is to use at least two or even three different words to describe how the character feels."

- "Today I want to teach you that once readers have identified strong feelings in a character, they analyze those feelings to understand more about that character. They ask themselves questions like, 'Why does this character have this emotion?' They can also think about what that emotion says about the character. Do the feelings seem exaggerated? Is the character acting in ways that display his or her feelings, or trying to hide them? Readers reread, looking for answers, and then support their conclusions with evidence from the text."

- "Often, in fairy tales, folktales, fables, and fantasy, the worlds the characters live in are significantly different from the world we live in. Today I want to teach you that readers try to make a picture in their mind of that world—what does it look like, what does it feel like to live in that world, how is it the same and how is it different from the world we live in?"

- "When readers get together to act out their stories, they can practice narrating a little bit of 'set-up,' describing the world where the story takes place. 'Once upon a time,' they might begin, 'in a land . . .' After all, if writers of fairy tales often do this—why shouldn't actors too?"

- "Today I want to teach you that readers pay close attention to the magic and other fantastical elements (imaginary creatures, talking animals and objects) in fairy tales, folktales, fables, and fantasy. Readers need to be able to understand how the magic in a story works, and one way to understand it is to dramatize it."

Use this list as a menu of possibilities, selecting only the teaching points that meet the needs of your students. Use your assessment data (running records, conferring and small-group notes, observations, responses to read-alouds, and other information) to decide on a plan that is tailored to the needs of your class. These teaching points may be used as whole-class minilessons, mid-workshop teachings, or for conferences and small-group work. You need not use every teaching point. See the unit overview for guidelines on how much time to spend in each bend.

- "Today I want to teach you that one way readers preserve their thinking about stories is by jotting it down as it occurs, on Post-its. They can then use their Post-its as conversation starters when they discuss the passage later with their partner."

- "Readers, today I want to remind you that readers not only pay attention to character feelings, they also try to understand a character's overall personality. One way to get to know a character is to look across your notes, looking for a pattern. When you see a pattern in the way a character acts, you have probably identified a trait of that character."

- "Today I want to teach you that readers, like directors, pay attention not only to *what* and *why* a character does things but also to *how* the character does these things. Does the book give any clues about the character's gestures? About the way a character walks or sits or closes the door? Readers (and directors) also pay attention to the way characters talk: the dialogue tags, the words they choose, their tone of voice, and the cues the author gives through dialogue. All of these give hints about what kind of people live in the world of a story."

BEND II: LITERARY LANGUAGE AND VOCABULARY

- "Readers, today we are not only going to be actors, we're also going to become storytellers! Before we can become great storytellers, we need to understand what it is that makes a great storyteller. Let's listen to some famous storytellers and do a mini-inquiry into what we notice. Then we'll have a chance to try it out ourselves!"

- "Today I want to teach you that sometimes authors use extra-special words, kind of like they are tugging on your shirtsleeve, saying 'Listen here!' Readers notice when an author has used extra-special words and make sure they understand what the author is trying to say or show."

- "Readers, today I want to teach you that sometimes an author will compare two things that are *very* different. As a reader, you have to stop and think, 'How are these two things alike? What is the author trying to say? What would make sense for the story?'"

- "Today I want to teach you that authors sometimes use playful language or words that can mean different things. It is up to the reader to use what's happening in the story and think about what would make sense, to figure out what the author meant."

- "Readers, today I want to remind you of the many strategies you know for figuring out tricky words. Remember though, it's not enough to simply figure out how to *say* the word. Careful readers read all around the word, before and after, for clues hinting at what the word might mean."

- "Today I want to teach you that it's not just the words that are tricky in fairy tales, folktales, fables, and fantasy—it's the sentences, too. Sometimes it's helpful to read longer, more complicated sentences in parts, breaking the sentence into smaller clusters of words, thinking about what each group of words means, and then rereading to put it all back together again. You can also look for signal words (like *if*, *or*, *but*) as places to break a sentence apart. Punctuation like commas and quotation marks for dialogue is also helpful for making sense of a longer sentence."

- "Today I want to teach you that readers use *everything* in combination to make sense of their stories and read with drama and expression. Think about all you know about how to read and make sense of stories, as well as what makes a great storyteller, when you are reading and acting out your fairy tales, folktales, fables, and fantasy."

BEND III: DISCOVERING PREDICTABLE ROLES CHARACTERS PLAY

- "Readers, by now you know a lot about how authors put characters together; you know that authors give characters wants and struggles, and personality traits and feelings. Today I want to teach you that as readers come to know something about how characters are created, they start to realize that particular types of characters pop up in lots of different books—and they read on the lookout for these types."

- "Today I want to teach you that readers consider the role of each character as they predict what's going to happen next. They might think, 'Who is the hero and who is the villain?' and 'What does this make me think about who will win and who will lose or what will happen next?'"

- "Today I want to teach you that when readers encounter a character type in a new book, they often think back on other books with the same character type. Readers ask themselves, 'How is this new character the same as and different from the characters in other books I have read?' This often leads to big ideas and questions that are interesting to talk about with a book club."

- "Readers, while fairy tales often include character types who are one-dimensional, in real life people are much more complicated. They are not 'all one way.' In real life, people might not be what they seem at first impression. They can have multiple sides to their personality, strengths and weaknesses, good and bad. Meanwhile, the evil characters in fairy tales are often just as ugly on the outside as they are on the inside, while the heroes and heroines are often beautiful and perfect in every way."

- "Today I want to teach you that you can always imagine new versions of fairy tales, folktales, and fables (or any book!), where there are more groups of people represented in the story. In your clubs, you can tell new versions of the stories you've read, changing the characters to make the story include groups of people that you haven't seen much in your books."

BEND IV: COMPARING AND CONTRASTING LESSONS THAT STORIES CONVEY

- "Today I want to teach you that readers learn lessons from the books they read. One way they can do this is by noticing what behaviors or actions contribute to a character's trouble and avoiding those behaviors in their own lives, or taking note of what kinds of things bring success, and using it to guide their own behavior."

- "Today I want to teach you that readers learn alongside the characters in their books. One way they might do this is by imagining how they will live their own lives differently because of what the characters have learned."

- "Today I want to teach you that some fairy tales, folktales, fables, and fantasy stories teach lessons with which we don't agree. As thoughtful readers, you need to do some critical thinking. Readers can think about whether a lesson doesn't ring true in their own world, and ask themselves, 'Do I agree with it?' or 'Does the good guy always win?' or 'Was that the best way to teach the lesson?' or 'Do I believe this is a good way to live my own life?'"

- "Today I want to teach you that readers compare and contrast books, thinking about how different authors convey the same lesson, or how different authors have opposing views on things."

- "Today I want to teach you that readers often think about books that go together: books that are versions of the same story, books that teach the same lessons, books that contain similar character types. Book clubs can work together to take all the books they've read and sort them into bins of books that go together. That way, other readers can find many books that they might be interested in, just by going to one basket or section of the library."